Also by Arlyn J. Macdonald

Essential Huna: Discovering and Integrating Your Three Selves

Nurturing the Inner Self: A Huna Approach to Wholeness

Parenting for Heart, Mind and Spirit: How to Effectively Parent Your Child, Your Self, and the Greater Community of Life

Celebrate!

Ceremonies and Blessings for Individuals, Families, and Spiritual Communities

ARLYN J. MACDONALD

ILLUSTRATED BY CATHARINE GATES

BALBOA.PRESS
A DIVISION OF HAY HOUSE

Balboa Press books may be ordered through booksellers or by contacting:

Balboa Press
A Division of Hay House
1663 Liberty Drive
Bloomington, IN 47403
www.balboapress.com
844-682-1282

ISBN: 978-1-9822-5517-6 (sc)
ISBN: 978-1-9822-5516-9 (e)

Print information available on the last page.

Balboa Press rev. date: 10/07/2020

Dedication

Thank you to all the friends and members of the Spiritual Awareness Center who have embraced these ceremonies and rituals as part of the celebrations of our spiritual family. This book is dedicated to each of you.

TABLE OF CONTENTS

Invitation xi

Introduction xiii

PERSONAL CEREMONIES AND RITUALS

Daily Rituals 1

    Greeting the Dawn 1

    Five Elements Breathing Meditation 2

    Breath of Light 2

    Evening Ritual 3

Personal Ceremonies 5

    Dedication to a New Spiritual Path 5

    Dedication of Your Life to Your Highest Good 7

    Name Changing Ceremony 8

    Self-Healing Ceremony 9

FAMILY CEREMONIES AND BLESSINGS

    Breaking Bread 15

    Mealtime Ritual 16

    Blessing of New Life (for the Mother and Father to Be) 16

    Blessing Way for Mother-To-Be 18

    The Song of Life (For Unborn Child) 22

    Naming Ceremony (Christening) 23

    Blessing of the Family 24

    Dedication Ceremony for Blending Families or Welcoming Adopted Children Into a Family 25

CEREMONIES AND BLESSINGS FOR LIFE CHANGES

Moonflower Ceremony for Girls 29

Way of the Wolf Ceremony for Boys 33

Wise Woman Ceremony 38

Wise Man Ceremony 42

Marriage and Commitment Ceremonies 46

Parting Ceremony 46

Blessing Home Ceremony 48

Memorial Ceremony with Rose Petal Ritual 49

COMMUNITY CEREMONIES AND BLESSINGS

Honoring Our Elders 55

Blessing of the Children 56

Blessing of the Women 58

Blessing of the Men 61

Blessing of the Animals 64

Community Healing Ceremony 65

Angel Blessing Ceremony 66

Dedication and Blessing Ceremony for Establishing a Community 67

CEREMONIES AND BLESSINGS FOR MOTHER EARTH

Earth Day Ceremony 73

Blessing of the Water 74

Blessing of the Trees 77

Blessing of the Fields 78

Blessing of the Garden 80

Blessing of the Rivers, Ponds, and Lakes 81

Blessing the Boats 82

CHANGING OF THE SEASONS

Spring Equinox Gathering 87

Summer Solstice Gathering 89

Autumn Equinox Gathering 91

Winter Solstice Gathering 92

CEREMONIES FOR HOLIDAYS

First Footer Ritual 97

New Year's – Burning Bowl Ceremony 97

White Stone Ceremony... 99

Easter Ceremony of Renewal Meditation and Dance.................... 100

Messengers of Light Ceremony 103

Ceremony of Remembrance... 109

Ceremony of Remembrance for Veterans Day................................ 110

CULTURAL AND RELIGIOUS CEREMONIES

Seder Ceremony – Jewish 115

Ho'oponopono Ceremony of Forgiveness – Hawaiian.................... 120

Wicca – Beltane Planting Ritual... 127

Lughnasa/Lammas Ritual 129

SPECIAL CEREMONIES

Home Cleansing, Blessing, and Dedication 133

Business Cleansing, Blessing, and Dedication............................... 135

Blessing of a Space to Transform Trauma Into Peace 137

Peace Pole Prayer Gatherings 138

Ceremony of Nations.. 138

CREATING YOUR OWN CEREMONIES

Wedding Ceremonies 144

Holy Union Ceremonies 146

Renewal of Marriage Vows 146

Suggestions for Additional Ceremonies to Create......................... 147

Appendix 149

Prayers to the Four Directions 149

Prayers to Release the Four Directions... 149

Sample Modern Seder Menu 150

Bibliography.. 151

INVITATION

You are invited to embark on a spiritual journey to rediscover the blessings of ritual and ceremony for yourself, your family, and your spiritual community. We are living in transformational times and many people are seeking new meaning in their lives. People have moved away from their spiritual lives and have become fragmented with materialism, coming to believe that only what we experience through the five senses is reality. But this physical reality is only a small part of the greater reality of life. It is time to return to balance and harmony and celebrate life once again.

Why is ceremony and ritual important? They are ways in which our hearts and minds come together with a spiritual focus to help reconnect us to the Divine Source of our being. Ceremonies are gateways or bridges into the spiritual realm, which we long for and desire on a soul level. Ceremonies draw us into another dimension where we once again experience our connection with the sacredness of life - our life and the life of all Creation.

Ritual and ceremony speak to the heart in a language not made of words, but of symbols and feelings, the true language of the heart and soul. They remind us of the goodness of life and reconnect us to the sacred, where we go beyond words and concepts to simply being. As Gabriel Horn says in *The Book of Ceremonies*, "Each prayer is a seed planted in the Mystery." Ceremonies, rituals, and blessing circles are prayer seeds planted in the spiritual realm inviting in the good of the individual, the family, and the greater community.

Ceremonies and rituals are living prayers. It is our responsibility to create these living prayers to enrich and enliven our lives. We wish you joy in using these ceremonies and hope they touch your hearts as they have touched ours.

The ceremonies and rituals in this book have become a part of the rich spiritual life of the Spiritual Awareness Center. They are designed to mark special times, to honor the best in us, and to guide us back to our inner life. Feel free to adapt these ceremonies in ways that make them sacred to you. Many of these ceremonies are based on Native American traditions. Use your own religious traditions or sacred symbols and prayers. Change them, relish them, enjoy them, but please keep them sacred.

Blessings,

Arlyn J. Macdonald

INTRODUCTION

Humans are not the only beings who create ceremony and ritual. Birds, lizards, and animals have rituals for bonding, mating, and mourning. For example, the setting sun affects both birds and animals. Sea gulls gather each evening on coastal rocks and sand to pay homage to the setting sun. In green jungles chimpanzees gather with their families to celebrate the setting sun and often leave papayas on the ground as offerings. There is a universal consciousness that draws all living beings to rituals and celebrations.

Humans are drawn to ceremony to experience a sense of peace and give more meaning to daily living. Ceremony brings us into intimate contact with the sacred in a very personal way. Not every ceremony speaks to individuals in the same way, but if we allow it to touch us, we will feel that deeper connection to the spiritual world. That is the purpose of ceremony, to make a profound impact, to pull us into a new place we may never have gone before, or to return us to a place of meaning.

Ceremonies are more formal acts celebrating important life events. Rituals are either a series of actions prescribed by a particular group or personal actions done in a sacred way to bring meaning to our lives.

There are religious and cultural ceremonies, family, community, national and global ceremonies. There are traditional and non-traditional ceremonies, ceremonies to encourage ideals, healing and honor ceremonies, and many other kinds. We even have our own personal ceremonies and rituals that affect us in subtle ways without our being conscious of them, such as where and when we drink our first cup of coffee in the morning. We have a vague sense of unease if we don't follow our personal rituals every day. All these rituals and ceremonies impact us in profound ways.

Even if ceremonies and rituals use different words or symbols, they all contain these essential elements. First, the ceremony is always done in a sacred way. It is a sacred bridge to allow participants to cross over and experience the spiritual meaning of the ritual. Second, each ceremony has a single intentional focus. Third, each ritual has symbols (lighting candles, sharing bread, exchanging rings, etc.) Symbols are the language of the heart and soul and are necessary to convey meaning without words. Fourth, spoken words, music, and actions are used to draw us into a different kind of experience. They help us pay attention, to be in a different reality where the sacred is working in and through us. And lastly, there is an element of blessing and thanksgiving that opens our hearts to be a channel for the Divine to work through to bring us to wholeness.

The ceremonies included in this book also draw on elements of traditional religions, Christianity, Judaism, Islam, Hinduism, Buddhism and other spiritual paths, as well as personal experience. They are meant to touch a deeper part of you and bring you healing. Whatever name you wish to use for GOD is exactly right for you, but the element of the Divine is important to include in the ceremony.

Every ceremony is a song and it is your voice that brings it to life. If you can add music or drumming to the ceremony, it will touch the heart in a deeper way. Many of the more formal rituals are based on Native American traditions that speak to our connection to Mother Earth.

From the deeply personal ceremonies to strengthen your own connection to the Divine, to the community and special ceremonies that bring people of all ages together, you will find at the heart of each ceremony a way to make each one meaningful to you. At the end of the book, you will find some tips on how to write your own ceremonies.

Ceremonies and rituals are gifts to encourage the sacred parts of us to come alive and join in the dance that crosses the bridge from the physical world to the spiritual and back again. Let them speak to you through the language of your heart.

Personal Ceremonies
and Rituals

Catharine Gates

DAILY RITUALS

※

Daily rituals are important for the individual. They connect us with the Great Mystery in a very personal way, speaking to our heart and spirit on the inner level. These Daily Rituals should be done at the same time and in the same manner each day with the understanding and intention that they are sacred. The rituals then become an important part of the weaving of your life, supporting and strengthening your connection with Spirit throughout the day.

GREETING THE DAWN

Supplies: Tobacco or Cornmeal or other offering.

Our wise Elders tell us that "We must never take from the world without expressing our gratitude and without giving something back." Therefore, every ritual to greet the dawn begins in gratitude. Native Americans and other traditional people greet each dawn with prayers and an offering of tobacco or cornmeal. Prayers of gratitude for your current blessings, prayers for the highest good of all beings, and guidance for you to do your best in this new day are important to contemplate at the beginning of each new day

Instructions: Gather your supplies and go outdoors, weather permitting, before the sun comes up. Remove your shoes and stand in the grass, if possible. Face East and stand in a relaxed position with your arms open or in prayer position in front of your heart. Let the rising sun flood your face with Light as you give thanks for the blessings of your life. Say the following prayer or one from your heart.

> *O, Great Spirit, I greet this new day you have given to me with gratitude for all my blessings. May I walk in beauty and harmony this day, respecting and being of service to my brothers and sisters, and to all beings. May I walk the path of good and if I should harm another by thought, word or deed, let me be quick to seek forgiveness and atonement. May I continue to have peace in my heart, in my words, and through my deeds. I pray for the well-being of our Mother the Earth and all her children. May all life be in balance and beauty. And, so it is.* (Add amen or a closing word signifying your prayer is finished.)

Breathe the energy of the new dawn into your prayer and when you feel in harmony with the new day, respectfully leave your offering to the Great Spirit. End your prayer facing the rising sun once more with hands in prayer position and bow in humbleness.

Notes: You may write your own prayer or find one that speaks to your heart. It is important in ceremonies and rituals to say the prayers out loud, so your heart can also listen to the sacred words.

FIVE ELEMENTS BREATHING MEDITATION

We are made of the elements of the cosmos. We are made of the same magnificence as the stars. Some traditions believe we once were each of the elements and carry that understanding in our DNA. This is a good ritual to return balance and wholeness to every part of us. It is important to not only think about the element as it is honored, but to feel what it is like to be the element.

Supplies: None.

Instructions: Go outdoors if the weather is good and remove your shoes to stand in the grass or on the ground facing the rising sun. Take a couple of deep breaths to bring yourself into harmony and balance. You will be taking five sets of five breaths each, in through the nose and out through the mouth with pursed lips (as if you were taking a long breath to gently blow out a candle.) As you take each breath, visualize one of the Five Elements that make up all of creation purifying your entire being- mind, heart, soul, and body. Take a rest between the sets and breathe easily and naturally for a few moments so you don't hyperventilate.

The first set of 5 breaths purifies with the Element of Earth.

The second set of 5 breaths purifies with the Element of Water.

The third set of 5 breaths purifies with the Element of Fire.

The fourth set of 5 breaths purifies with the Element of Air.

The fifth set of 5 breaths purifies with the Element of Ether (the subtle element).

> *By the Earth that is my Body; by the Water that is my Soul; by the Fire that is my Heart; by the Air that is my Mind; by the Subtle Element that is my Higher Self; I now affirm the Wholeness of my creation and the Oneness of All That Is. And, so it is!*

End your breath meditation with a prayer of gratitude and appreciation for all the Elements that form this wonderful world of creation, including you.

BREATH OF LIGHT

Each breath you take is an exchange of energy with the rest of the world. Your breath is important in helping to maintain Love, Joy and Peace around you. Each time you breathe these Truths out into the world, they begin the journey to encircle the planet and return to you. It is important to always be mindful of your breath.

Supplies: None.

Instructions: Go to a quiet place where you won't be disturbed for a few minutes. Begin by breathing deeply, in through the nose and out through the mouth until the rhythm of your breathing becomes calm and peaceful. When your breathing is calm, use your visualization and begin to breathe in Light and breathe out Love. Do this as many times as necessary to begin to feel Love. Take a few more breaths to increase the feeling of Love. When you are filled with Love, with the next breath, breathe in Light and breathe out Joy. Continue to breathe in Light and breathe out Joy until you begin to feel joyful. Continue to breathe in this manner until you are joyful. When you are joyful, take a new breath breathing in Light and breathing out Peace. Continue to breathe in Light and breathe out Peace until you feel completely in your Center of Peace and every part of your body feels calm and peaceful. When you are at peace, return to the present moment.

> *I set my intention now to make every breath I take a holy breath. I will breathe in Light and breathe out Love, Joy and Peace to all I meet. And, so it is.*

Notes: It is important that you bring the feelings of Love, Joy and Peace to this breathing meditation to meld mind and heart to your breath and become as one.

EVENING RITUAL

The last thoughts we have before we go to sleep are the ones our subconscious mind works on through the night. This is the reason we often wake up to a solution or a new idea about the challenge we were thinking of when we went to sleep. This time is also our opportunity to release any hurtful situations and ask forgiveness of ourselves for not seeing a situation or a person through the eyes of Truth.

Supplies: None.

Instructions: Reserve time for yourself after you get ready for bed and the time you turn off the light to go to sleep. During this time, take some centering breaths until you feel calm and relaxed. Bring to your mind any situation that occurred during the day about which you felt uneasy or troubled. Reflect on the situation and recognize any part you had in making the situation more difficult. Call on your spiritual self to show you ways to make amends the following day to move towards resolution. Ask forgiveness of yourself that you did not see what was happening and pledge to listen more carefully to and be mindful of your inner guidance. Release the situation to its highest good.

After asking forgiveness and releasing the situation, invite the Divine Spirit into your life. Fill your thoughts with something positive you want to accomplish, a spiritual principle you wish to increase in your life, or thanksgiving for all your blessings. Your subconscious mind takes over the minute you fall asleep and you will awaken in the morning rested, feeling good, and with a great new idea or new resolution.

I now release everything in my day that did not serve my highest good. I ask forgiveness for not seeing the Truth and I pledge to wake up in the morning with a glad and joyful heart, knowing that I am guided to my highest good. I am so grateful to God for all my blessings. And, so it is.

Notes: The act of forgiving yourself is an important part of the forgiveness process. We are asking forgiveness of our heart-self that we did not realize the Truth about the situation.

PERSONAL CEREMONIES

Personal ceremonies, are more formal rituals, performed when we want to honor the sacredness of a change in our life, to mark an important event, or to reaffirm that we are spiritual beings. Many life changing events are traditionally marked with ceremonies, but there are many other times when a personal ceremony is needed but is not necessarily accessible. Personal ceremonies are based on a person's own religious or spiritual views and can be performed alone or with friends and family. Personal ceremonies contain symbols and meanings for the emotions as well as the mind. The symbols are uniquely personal, representing a deeper meaning for the individual. A person may also ask another person to lead the ceremony. Personal ceremonies often materialize out of dreams, insights, or prayers.

You might also want to create a ceremony for an important life event you wanted to mark but couldn't at the time. You can always do ceremony at any time for any important moment in your life.

DEDICATION TO A NEW SPIRITUAL PATH

Often in our lives we grow out of old beliefs into new ones. We might change religions or adopt a new way of living spiritually. To mark this important life changing event, a special ceremony can be created. It is important that all the symbols used are positive and represent the new way of believing. It is also important that no negative thoughts or feelings about an old path influence the ceremony. This is a celebration of a new understanding about life and Spirit.

Supplies: A special cloth for an altar; a candle and matches; a small container filled with pure water that has been blessed, which is the symbol of the new spiritual path; other meaningful symbols; and flowers in a small vase. Special scriptures, readings, or music can be included. Prepare yourself for this ceremony to make it sacred. Come to the ceremony with a clean body and symbolically wash your hands before beginning the ritual.

Instructions: Choose a sacred place to hold this ceremony. It can be outdoors or indoors. Spread the altar cloth on the ground or on a small table. Arrange the candle, container of water, and other symbols, and the vase of flowers in a sacred manner. Let your heart-self guide you as to the placement.

Prepare yourself by taking a few deep breaths and bringing yourself to peace. Start your special music and light the candle. Be in a state of sacredness as you open your heart to let the Divine fill your body, mind, and emotions. When you are ready, say the first prayer out loud in a sacred manner. You may place your hands in prayer position or open your arms for the prayers.

> *Today, I am a new person with a new spiritual purpose in life. I call upon the Angels, Guides, and Teachers to be with me as I take this first step toward my new life. I invite my Higher Self and the Holy Spirit to be present with me here as I dedicate my life to my new purpose.*

Read any special scriptures or readings you have chosen for inspiration for your new path.

Bless the water with a prayer holding your hands over the container. Dip your fingers into the blessed water and gently touch each of the symbols you have placed on your altar cloth. As you bless them, dedicate your life to the ideals they represent. Then dip your fingers into the water again to bless and dedicate yourself to your new spiritual life as follows:

Bless your new insight by touching the middle of your forehead.

> *My thoughts are now dedicated to Peace.*

Bless your new expression by touching your lips.

> *My words are now dedicated to speaking words of Love.*

Bless your new clarity by touching your throat.

> *My intentions are now dedicated to the Highest Good for all.*

Bless your new feelings of Compassion by touching your heart.

> *My heart is now dedicated to reach out only with Love.*

Bless your new spiritual purpose by touching your solar plexus.

> *My body is now dedicated to Right Actions.*

Read the final prayer, or say one from your heart, to mark this sacred time.

> *I release my body into Light. I release my mind into Peace. I release my heart into Love. I release my Soul into the Sacred. I release my steps to walk this new holy path. And, so it is.*

Spend as much time as you like in the silence, integrating this ceremony into your whole being. When you are ready, blow out your candle and either drink the remaining water or pour it out on your front threshold as a symbol that each time your foot passes over your threshold to step out into the world, you are stepping onto your new spiritual path.

Note: You may also want to remove your shoes each time you step from the outside world into your own sacred home, if you haven't already been doing so.

DEDICATION OF YOUR LIFE TO YOUR HIGHEST GOOD

This is a very private and sacred ceremony to dedicate your heart and mind, body and spirit to walking the sacred path. At some point in a person's life, he or she is awakened to a deep calling to follow the sacred. This calling comes at different ages for different people. Only you can hear the call and only you can answer it. It is the call to recognize your life is sacred and the answer is your commitment to be the holy being you were meant to be.

When you decide to answer the call, you may want to do a sacred ceremony that blesses your new life.

Supplies: A sacred place in nature; new white candle and lighter (Fire); new sacred symbol as a gift to yourself (necklace, pendant, bracelet, statue, etc.); sage; special red cloth for altar; bowl of pure water (Water); fresh flowers; hard-boiled egg; anointing oil or olive oil in small container; a stone (Earth); and, a feather (Air). Your declaration affirming your choice to follow the sacred path written out.

PURIFICATION OF THE BODY: The evening before the ceremony do not eat anything after 8:00 p.m. Take a shower and wash your hair.

PURIFICATION OF THE HEART: The day before, make amends to someone you have caused harm to and ask for and receive forgiveness.

PURIFICATION OF THE MIND: Meditate on gratitude in the early morning hours for 3 days before the ceremony.

PURIFICATION OF THE SPIRIT: Go to the sacred place you have chosen to do the ceremony 2 days before and spend 1-2 hours in prayer.

Instructions: Go to the sacred place and arrange your special items on your red cloth. If you can do this ceremony by a river or lake, it will increase your blessings. Remove your shoes and socks. Light the sage and smudge your entire body. Sit down on the ground in front of your altar and light your candle. (If it goes out during the ceremony, that is okay as it is symbolic of bringing in the Light.) Spend some time in meditation calming your thoughts and emotions and filling your being with peace.

Invitation to Your Higher Self

Beloved Higher Self, heavenly Spirit who loves and guides us, be with us, heart and mind, as we dedicate ourselves to walking in beauty and following the sacred path of life. (You may also invite in the Angels, Guides, Teachers, etc. you are connected to, so they can also be a part of your ceremony.)

Declaration of Intention

When you feel the presence of the Sacred Beings and your Higher Self, make your declaration out loud, say it with great conviction and meaning. (You can write your own or use the following. Remember you are speaking from the consciousness of your heart and mind and body to your soul)

We declare that we are ready to receive and accept our sacred purpose to walk this sacred path. We dedicate our life to accomplish this sacred purpose and to strive to listen to the inspirations of Spirit, to be mindful of our thoughts and uplift them to the sacred realms, to speak life-affirming words of support, kindness and compassion, and to be the Light of Peace in all our actions. We choose to work for the highest good of all, including ourselves, and to serve the greatest need. We will treat our body as the sacred temple it is, caring for it, nurturing it, and loving it. All of these promises and more do we affirm in this dedication. May it be pledged today and forever more. And, so it is.

Peel the egg and bless it. Slowly eat the egg as a symbol of partaking of your new life, savoring each bite, honoring the gift of renewal. Bless the bowl of water and the anointing oil and the symbol of your dedication. Take a sip of the pure water, remembering you are drinking the message of your dedication into your body. Pour the remaining water over your bare feet as a symbol that your understanding of the sacred purpose for your life is clear. Anoint yourself rising to the level of your Higher Self, first on your crown, center of your brow, each eye lid, your nose, mouth and chin. Then anoint your throat, heart, solar plexus, sacral and base chakras. (You may use the sign of the equidistant cross or a spiral for the anointing).

Lift up the symbol of your dedication to Father Sky and down to Mother Earth and say:

We accept this gift, both heart and mind, as a symbol of our dedication to our new sacred path. May it remind us always that we now stand in the Light of Spirit and we have all the resources and guidance to follow this path.

Put the necklace, etc. around your neck. Place your hands in prayer position holding them first at your heart, then to your lips, and then to your brow.

In sacredness it is finished. May I walk in sacredness and share the sacredness of Spirit with all the world. And, so it is.

NAME CHANGING CEREMONY

For many people, the name they were born to, and called by family, no longer serves the highest purpose for their life. Names are sometimes changed when a person chooses a different religion, wants to express higher aspects of themselves, or when a new name is given to them through another ritual or a dream. Careful thought should be given to a name change. Names are powerful expressions of inner spiritual energy. Meanings of the new name are important. It is sometimes helpful to research the meaning of the new name. The mind and heart should whole-heartedly agree to the new name. This ceremony can be done alone or with a loving and supportive group.

Supplies: Paper and pen, a candle and matches, and an article of jewelry with new name engraved on it. (For example, a locket for women, a bracelet for men or women, a key chain ornament that can be engraved.)

Instructions: Prepare yourself to receive the new name by releasing all the old thoughts and feelings about the old name before the ceremony. Gather at or go to a place that is sacred to you. Set up the candle in a safe place and light it. Bless the symbol of your new name by holding it above the candle and circling the candle three times. Set the blessed symbol to the side.

Open yourself to becoming a new person, to becoming more of who you really are. Write your full old name on a piece of paper. Fold up the paper and taking it in both hands, close your hands around it. Walk around the candle in a circle counterclockwise three times saying:

> *I release the past and I honor the person I thought I was. I release the past and I honor the person I felt I was. I am no longer this person. I am no longer this person. I am not longer this person.*

When you have completed the three circles, take the paper and carefully light it on fire with the candle's flame. Let it burn completely. If there is any ash, place it reverently in a small hole in Mother Earth to be transformed.

Take the new article and holding it to your heart, walk around the circle three more times this time going clockwise and saying:

> *I am now (new full name). I take this new name as a symbol of my higher purpose in life. I accept all the positive truths of my new name and I dedicate myself to expressing these truths in my thoughts, words, and deeds. I am now (new full name).*

When you have completed the circles, place the symbol around your neck or on your wrist. Say a prayer of gratitude of your own or the following to seal your new name.

> *As I place this symbol on my body, it is a reminder to me that I choose to be a new person with a new name that expresses more clearly my higher purposes. I am so very grateful to (the Divine) and my Higher Self for inspiring me to be more of who I really am. I thank my parents for my birth name that was just right for me at the time and I will always honor that name and their contributions to my life. I am grateful for my life. And, so it is.*

SELF-HEALING CEREMONY

All ceremonies have an element of self-healing. All healing begins with forgiveness. Before using this ceremony, spend some time reviewing your life to see if there are any new hurts or old hurts that need forgiving, especially those hurts done to your own self. Your heart-self is the part of you that is injured, most often when we do not act in a mindful and respectful way towards our emotional self. We forget that we need to ask for forgiveness from ourselves.

Aches and pains in the body are messages from the inner self that we are not paying attention to thoughts and feelings that need healing. One way to discover the area in need is to read Louise Hay's book, "Heal Your Body A-Z." In this remarkable book, she correlates specific ailments to the thought behind it and then adds a positive affirmation to help in the healing.

If you have studied symbols and their meanings, you might also discover the area of your life that needs healing. For instance, feet represent "understanding." If you have feet problems you may be misunderstanding a truth about yourself, your life, or others. A positive affirmation to use might be, "I see clearly now, I understand the truth."

Supplies: Altar cloth, candle and matches, light massage oil or olive oil in small bowl. Soothing inspirational music to play in the background. Affirmations or a meditation for healing.

Instructions: If you have not done the self-forgiveness process, go back and do it before you begin. You want heart, mind, and spirit to be in alignment for this ceremony and for your healing.

Create a quiet space for yourself either indoors or outdoors. Spread your altar cloth on the ground or on a small table. Place the candle and bowl of oil on the altar cloth. Close your eyes and bring yourself to your Center of Peace breathing deeply for a few moments. When you are at peace, light the candle and start the music. Continue to breathe deeply for a few more moments, open your eyes and read your positive affirmations or do a meditation for healing. Then begin with a prayer:

I humbly ask that my Divine Higher Self, my Angels, Guides, and Teachers be with me for this healing. I know that they stand beside me as I affirm for me and my Heart Self: I am whole, complete and perfect. I am now in perfect alignment with my body, heart, and mind. I am being blessed with the healing Light of my Divine Higher Self.

Picture healing Light entering the top of your head and completely filling your body with healing and sacred energy. Direct this healing Light to the part of your body that you want to heal. Continue visioning this Light filling every cell and every atom of your physical body until it spills over into your spiritual body. See your body start to glow with radiant healing Light. Feel yourself uplifted into pure healing energy. This is your true body – a body of Light. There is no place in your true body of Light that is not perfect. You are whole, complete, and perfect.

Place your hand over the bowl of oil and bless it.

I bless this oil in the name of my Divine Higher Self. It is a gift of healing.

Take a small amount of oil on your fingertips and massage it gently onto the part of you that needs healing as is practical. Or simply touch the spot making a spiral design with the oil. Repeat the beginning prayer two additional times.

Take a few moments more to breathe into your healing. Know that you are forgiven and healed. Picture your Light body again and how it feels to be Light. Stay in this feeling until it begins to fade.

Thank your Divine Self, your Heart Self, your Angels, Guides and Teachers for being a part of this Healing Ceremony. Place your hands at prayer position and with a bowed head, say "Thank you" and repeat the following affirmation.

I am now healed, whole, complete, and perfect.
You are now healed, whole, complete, and perfect.
(Your name) is now healed, whole, complete, and perfect.
And, so it is now and forever more.

Blow out the candle, turn off the music, and take a deep breath of gratitude.

Note: A Community Healing ceremony can be found in the *Community* section.

Family Ceremonies and Blessings

FAMILY CEREMONIES

Family is the perfect setting for sacred ceremonies and blessings. Families naturally develop ceremonies and rituals and every family member can participate in them from grandparents to the children. Family is our first school, where we learn what it is to be a social human being, how to treat each other, and how to treat ourselves. Family is where we first learn to honor the sacred in everything, to respect Mother Earth, and to remember our connection to the Great Divine Mystery.

BREAKING BREAD

Traditionally the breaking and sharing of bread is part of the blessing of a meal and comes from ancient times. The actual breaking of the loaf and passing it around to each person present at the meal is symbolic of our connection with each other and with the Divine who provides sustenance to us all. There are many formal ceremonies such as the sacred act of communion offered in churches, where bread and wine served together have religious meanings. There are also informal rituals among family members and friends that symbolize the sharing of not only the physical qualities of nurturing the body, but the spiritual qualities of nurturing the soul.

Bread is a combination of earthly ingredients enlivened with yeast, which symbolizes the Holy Spirit enlivening our lives. Bread is an ancient symbol for truth. Truth is the spiritual food for the soul. It refreshes our minds and hearts in a very physical way as the sugar in the starches of the grain act immediately on our bodies.

In whatever way you share or break bread, the meaning is the same. It is a deeper understanding of the connection between our inner soul and the outer world. It is an affirmation of the bond between all humanity and the Divine.

Supplies: A small loaf of bread cut almost in half and placed on a special plate.

Instructions: Gather the family and guests around the table before the meal.

Leader: We join our ancestors and people all over the world who break bread and to give thanks for the fruits of the earth given us by our Creator to sustain our lives. We break bread together to give thanks for our family, our friends and all our blessings.

Hold up the loaf of bread: *This bread feeds our body and is a symbol for the truth that feeds our souls. When the grains and the leavening are mixed together, they become something more – they became something new – the bread. When we eat the bread remembering it is symbolic of truth, we also become something new.*

Break the loaf in half completely and pass around one half, the other half is placed back on the plate and served with the meal: *Take a portion of this bread of life and remember that you are more than what you think you are. Every time you eat of this bread, you are made new. Let us give thanks for the blessings of each other, for all of our beloved family members, all of our dear friends, and most of all let us give thanks for the Creator who has given us life.*

Everyone takes a portion of the bread and eats it in a respectful manner.

Note: The breaking of the bread may be followed by a grace or the meal.

MEALTIME RITUAL
(courtesy of Catharine Gates)

The purpose of this ritual is to bring peace and gratitude to each meal and to acknowledge the Divine purpose of food which is to nourish our body.

Supplies: A candle and lighter.

Instructions: Light the candle, repeat the prayer, dedication and ending.

Blessing

Divine Mystery, thank you for this bounty before us. Bless this food to its use and us to thy service. Thank you.

We light a candle to remind us of Your light and the peace that You have bestowed on us.

Thank you, Divine Source, for blessing us with this food. We go out from here with a nourished body and a happy, grateful heart. And, so it is.

BLESSING OF NEW LIFE
(For the Mother and Father to Be)

This is a private ceremony to honor the new mother and father who have come together to celebrate the greatest mystery – the creation of a new life. It is a reverent ritual to mark the sacredness of the experience of bringing new life into the world and to bless the parents to be with clarity and understanding.

Supplies: A flower bud symbolizing the new life, four votive candles and lighter, pure water in a bowl.

Instructions: Find a sacred place outdoors, if possible. Place the votive candles in each of the four directions with the flower bud in the center. Place the bowl of water to the side. The couple stands facing each other holding hands and the ceremony begins with the couple saying this prayer or other appropriate prayer together.

Opening Prayer

Divine Mystery, we come to this place and time to honor each other and the holy life that has been created from our bodies and our spirits and our love. As this new life was created in Love, we affirm that we will nurture and protect this new life with our love. In your Holy Name we promise that we will care for each other with compassion and kindness, recognizing that we have two different roles to play in the shaping of our child's life and that we will lavish love and affection on each other and on this holy child. It is Love that will guide our actions in all things. We call upon the Four Directions, which represent aspects of the Divine Mystery (God) to guide us as we become mother and father to this child.

Father lights the first candle that sits in the East while the mother repeats this prayer:

Spirit of the East, the direction of new beginnings, be with us as we learn how to guide our child with patience with each other and this tiny life. Help us to remember it is the small things that shape our lives.

Mother lights the second candle that sits in the South while the father repeats this prayer:

Spirit of the South, the direction of learning, be with us as we learn to be loving parents and as we teach the knowledge of mind, heart and spirit to our child.

Father lights the third candle that sits in the West, while the mother repeats this prayer:

Spirit of the West, the direction of actions, be with us as we become more mindful of our actions towards each other and toward our child. Help us be mindful that each action comes from our gentleness, even in times of stress.

Mother lights the fourth candle that sits in the North, while the father repeats this prayer.

Spirit of the North, the direction of reflection, be with us as we take time to be in the silence alone and together to bring balance and harmony into our family life and to teach this child the beauty of the quiet.

The couple then blesses the pure water by putting their hands over the bowl and saying a personal prayer of blessing. The father and then the mother dip their fingers into the bowl of water and touches the forehead, heart and palms of the hands of the other person while saying the blessing:

I bless you, your mind and your thoughts that they find the best way to care for our child.

I bless you, your heart and your feelings that will bring only laughter and happiness to our new family.

I bless you, your hands and your actions that will care for yourself, for me, and for our child with strength and kindness.

The flower bud is then dipped into the bowl of water as a symbol of blessing the unborn child and presented to the Four Directions. Then the remaining water is spilled onto the ground to return to Mother Earth as a blessing. The candles are blown out with gratitude to the Four Directions.

The ceremony ends with a gentle kiss to seal the blessings and promises. (The flower bud may be pressed in a large book between two sheets of paper and when dry saved in the Baby's Book or other keepsake album.)

BLESSING WAY FOR MOTHER-TO-BE

In America, we traditionally celebrate a coming birth with a baby shower. The shower welcomes the new life through the gathering of friends and family and the giving of gifts. However, a baby shower does not usually include a sacred element. The mystery of new life is the most sacred of all acts. Women who have experienced the Blessing Way ceremony report they did not realize they would be participating in such a holy time and that being blessed made them feel sacred and deeply connected to the miracle of birth.

This formal ceremony is based on the Blessingway ritual of the Navajo people. The Blessing Way honors the divine procreative powers. It helps establish a spiritual bond between the mother and the women of her family and her friends. It honors the eternal Sisterhood of all Women through the Goddess. The Blessing Way also blesses the path for the child soon to be born and opens the mother to the special magic of birth. It is a gift for all who participate, as we are all a part of the Great Circle of Life, connected to the Great Mother and to each other. (Men may also be included in this ceremony, but not in the Weaving of the Mothers.)

Supplies: A small basket with paper and pencils for writing out blessings for the mother and child; ball of red yarn and scissors; a flower wreath with red ribbons for the mother-to-be. Place a small table with special cloth in the center of the gathering; blessing oil or olive oil in a small bowl in the center of the table; small bunch of flowers and a green votive candle placed in the East; a seashell and a blue votive candle in the South; a small statue of a horse and a red votive candle in the West; a small statue of a white bear and a white votive candle in the North; and a lighter. Gifts may be brought by the participants. Refreshments may be served after the ceremony.

Instructions: This ceremony has three parts: Ritual of Connection and the Honoring of Our Mothers; the Prayers and Blessings of the Four Directions; and the Blessing of the Mother-to-Be and

All Women. The Leader asks four women to represent the Four Directions and light the candle for her direction and to read the prayer for that direction.

As the guests enter the room or outdoor space, they are invited to write out a blessing for the family and place it in the basket. Later in the quiet, the mother-to-be will take each blessing and read it to her unborn child in remembrance of this sacred time.

When the ceremony begins, place the flower wreath on the head of the mother-to-be. It can be placed by the oldest or youngest woman present. Seat her in a place of honor.

Opening

Leader: *Welcome. We come together to bless (Name) as she begins the journey of bringing this holy child into the world. This is a holy act and all women are a part of it. We honor (Name) as a symbol of the Holy Mother of us All.*

Blessing Prayer

Leader*: Let us pray. Holy Mother of all Life, we come here today to honor you through honoring womanhood. We acknowledge your presence as Mother Earth, from whence all life springs. We honor your presence in this new life that (Mother-to-Be) will soon bring into this world. We ask your blessing on this mother, on this unborn child and on the father. We ask your blessings on all the women (and men) gathered here in your name. And, so it is.*

The Weaving of the Mothers

Leader: *We are unlike any other creature on earth. We use this ritual of connection to remind us of our sisterhood, our uniqueness, and in honor of our power of creation. This red ball of yarn is a symbol of the special bond that connects all women, stronger than the tie of blood. As the yarn is passed to you, wrap a loop around your wrist in honor of each female ancestor whose name you know, reciting their names. (I am [Name], the daughter of [Name], who is the daughter of [Name], etc.) Keeping the yarn connected, pass the ball of yarn to the next woman. As the names are spoken, let each past mother be honored who has brought us here to this place and time. The Mother-to-Be will be the last woman to name her mothers.*

When all the names have been recited and all are connected in this symbol of the web of life, the Leader asks for a few moments in the silence to send energy and love to all the female ancestors. Then scissors are passed around with instruction to cut enough yarn to tie a knot and secure the yarn bracelet around the wrist. The bracelets may be worn to remember the connection of all women and the honoring of all our mothers. (Leader begins with her mothers' names.)

The Prayers and Blessings of the Four Directions

Leader: *Will the four women who are representing the Four Directions come forward to read the prayers and blessings and light their candles?*

Prayer to the East - *We ask the wisdom of the East to be present with us today – the spirit of air, of spring, and the energy of the rising sun. We bring Flowers to represent spring and we light the green candle for the Spirit of the East.*

We ask that this mother (and this father) be blessed with the beauty of this new life and new beginning. May the pregnancy and birth of their child deepen their connection to each other, to the Creator, to their families and to this holy child. May they feel God's hand in this miracle of birth.

May this sacred child be secure in the love of the parents, family and friends as this new life enters the world with grace and joy. May (Mother-to-Be) be strengthened by her holy breath as she brings forth this new life. We thank you, wisdom of the East.

Prayer to the South - *We ask the wisdom of the South to be present with us today – the spirit of water, of summer and the energy of the noonday sun. We bring a Seashell to represent water and we light the blue candle for the Spirit of the South.*

We ask that this mother (and this father) be blessed with childlike wonder. May the spirit of their baby open them to joy and spontaneity. We ask special blessing for this tiny spark of life now grounded to the nurturing earth below. May this child feel the love of family and friends all the days of his or her life.

May this child always remember the important connection to and the love of the Divine. May this child's heart always be open to see the good. May the spirit of the Dolphin watch over this child, blessing the birth as the child emerges from the water of the womb. We thank you, wisdom of the South.

Prayer to the West - *We ask the wisdom of the West to be present with us today – the spirit of fire, of autumn and the energy of the setting sun. The brilliance of fire and autumn are represented by this Horse and we light the red candle for the Spirit of the West.*

We ask that this mother (and this father) be blessed with the experience of creativity through the power of this birth. May they be blessed with the passion of the West and may their relationship deepen and grow stronger through the birth of their holy child, the beginning of their sacred family.

We ask special blessings for (Father-to-Be). May the birth of his child open him to the miracle of life and new expressions of joy and love. May his connection to the Divine grow even stronger and may the spirit of the Horse help him to be a strong companion and partner at this birthing, as he takes on the important role of fatherhood. May the spirit of the Horse strengthen him so that he can strengthen (Mother-to-Be) to bring their child into the world. We thank you, wisdom of the West.

Prayer to the North - *We ask the wisdom of the North to be present with us today – the spirit of earth, of winter, the luminosity of the moon, introspection, and of the time we all spend in the darkness of the womb. Earth is represented by the White Bear and we light the white candle for the Spirit of the North.*

We ask that the strength of the Bear support (Mother-to-Be) as she opens to this powerful experience of birth. We ask that the peace of Mother Earth be with her as her body and heart move together in the dance of life and her mind be stilled with peace. We ask that the strength of the Bear also be with (Father-to-Be) as he becomes the pillar of strength for his family. May these last days of pregnancy and expectation be a time for deep introspection for both parents as they prepare for the changes that new life brings. We thank you, wisdom of the North.

Ritual Blessing for the Women

Leader: *As we have honored and blessed our mothers and their mothers, we now bless ourselves by blessing our own sacred bodies. I will be using anointing oil to bless (Mother-to-Be). I invite you to do a self-blessing, touching the different parts of your own body as I recite the words of blessing. I will pass the anointing oil if you would like to use a drop for your blessing.*

> *Bless me Mother,*
> *Bless my eyes to behold only beauty around me,*
> *Bless my nose to smell the sweet essence of life,*
> *Bless my lips to speak only good and healing words,*
> *Bless my ears to hear the cry of those in need,*
> *Bless my breasts, that I may comfort and sustain life,*
> *Bless my womb that my creativity may grow strong and flourish,*
> *Bless my source of creation, that brings forth life for good,*
> *Bless my hands to do your sacred work,*
> *Bless my feet to walk on the straight path of honor,*
> *Bless my heart to know your wisdom.*
> *Thank you, Holy Mother, for being with me always. Your Love and Light sustain and protect me.*
> *Thank you for the abundant blessings of my life.*
> *Bless me, Mother, for I am your sacred child and your holy woman. (Bring hands to prayer position)*

Leader: *Will the Women of the Four Directions please blow out your candles as I speak the closing prayers?*

As the Spirit of the North leaves us, we ask that your solitude and peacefulness be with us as we prepare for the challenges ahead. Thank you for your presence. We release you now.

As the Spirit of the West leaves us, we ask your energy and creativity to inspire us to new ways of living and being. Thank you for your presence. We release you now.

As the Spirit of the South leaves us, may we find ourselves open to trust the innocent spirit each of us was born with. We release you now.

As the Spirit of the East leaves us, let us soar upon the rays of light to new beginnings, trusting our intuition to guide us. We release you now.

May we find our lives blessed with the connections of sisterhood and blessed through this new life to be born into a world of love. And, so it is.

Go now in peace (Name) blessed with the wisdom of the Spirits of the Four Directions and the Power of the Holy Mother who will stand beside as you fulfill her Love, bringing this sacred life into this community of Love. And, so it is.

THE SONG OF LIFE (FOR UNBORN CHILD)
(Based on a traditional African ritual)

This is a ceremony based on a traditional African ritual that comes from honoring the Divine Goddess of Birth and includes the whole community. When a woman knows she is pregnant, she invites her close friends to go out into nature with her where they pray and meditate together until they hear the song of the unborn child. Each soul has its own song. The women stay together until the song manifests.

When the song comes, and the women have learned it, they return to the family/community and teach it to everyone else. When the child is born, the parents sing the song to the newborn. When the family gathers for the first time with the newborn, they sing the song. The song is sung to the child on each special life transition, including the initiation into adulthood and marriage. When the person is about to pass from this world, the family and friends sing the person into the next life with his or her Song of Life.

There is another occasion during which the song is sung. If the child at any time during his or her life commits a crime or a hurtful social act, the individual is called to stand in the middle of a circle of the community and his/her song is sung to remind the person who he or she really is. This is done in recognition that the correction for this kind of behavior is not punishment, but love and the remembrance of our true identity, which is spiritual, not physical.

Supplies: Pregnant woman, close friends, guitar and drums(optional) and a beautiful spot in nature.

Instructions: Choose a beautiful and secluded place in nature. Invite the pregnant woman and her close friends to spend time together with the purpose of discovering the Song of Life for the unborn child. Gather with the purpose of being quiet and listening and a commitment to discover and learn the song before returning home. Form a circle and say the following prayer or one written for the occasion to begin this ritual.

Opening

Leader: *Bless us, Mother, for we are your children and your representatives on this earth. Be with us as we honor this new expression of the Divine soon to be born into our circle. We stand open to hear the voice of Truth for this new child. Send the Song of Life to us as emissaries of your wisdom. May we be in serenity and peace and love. Guide us to receive for this child, the beautiful music of his or her soul that this song may sustain and nourish the soul of this child as it grows in strength and purpose. Amen. And, so it is.*

Spend as much time as needed to listen in the quiet and share any music that comes. Be creative and inspired. Write down the song or sing it into a recorder so it will be remembered. Sing the song at the baby's birth and other important occasions.

NAMING CEREMONY
(CHRISTENING)

Naming a baby is a sacred act. A name carries all the hopes and dreams of the parents, as well as the inspiration for the child's life. The name intones the vibrational energies in the newborn baby. Many religious traditions mark the naming ceremony (christening) as the first ritual or sacrament of life. A naming ceremony may be held in a religious place or it may be held outdoors or at home. Some traditions require godparents be chosen and attend the naming ceremony. These are special people who are responsible for the spiritual upbringing of their godchild.

A naming ceremony is also a ritual to open the spiritual centers of the new child, surrounded by the protective love of his or her parents and family. Parents may also want the ceremony to include dedicating the child to God. It can be a private ceremony, or include extended family, or all the members of a spiritual community.

Most religious leaders want to have a conversation with the parents and godparents about the significance of the naming ceremony (christening) prior to the event.

Supplies: Small bowl of pure water blessed by the leader or minister or parents. Rose petals may be floated on top of the water if desired; and, a small table (optional.)

Instructions: Have the water ready on a small table or have someone hold it during the ceremony. The leader may take the baby in his or her arms for the ceremony or the baby may stay in the arms of another designated person representing a spiritual presence. Words used in this naming ceremony are not as important as the symbols and prayers. (If the baby cries during the ceremony, continue the service. The crying means the baby is sensitive to what is really going on.)

Leader: *Welcome. We are gathered here today to celebrate the naming of this child and the blessing of his (her) spirit. This ceremony is symbolic of helping to strengthen the physical body, align the emotions, and activate the higher body of light of the child's soul. We invite the Angels, especially the Guardian Angel of this child, to be here with us now and throughout this child's life.*

We were born to be a sacred people, manifesting the Light of God (the Divine) within us. May we be blessed with the Love of the Divine as we come together now to bless this child, this new soul, and activate his/her body of Light.

Charge to Parents and Grandparents

Will you, (names), parents of this child, affirm your commitment to nurture and love him/her all the days of your life? (We will.)

Will you, (names), godparents of this child, affirm your commitment to help this child on his or her chosen spiritual path and to be as second parents to him/her? (We will.)

Will all of you gathered here as representatives of the greater family of this child, affirm your commitment to support, teach and love this child? (We will).

O Great Creator of us all, we acknowledge your great presence in this moment; may your Light infuse the physical body of this child; nurture the emotional body and inspire the mental body with health, wisdom, and inner vitality. May this child find peace in your presence, love with his/her family, and guidance and comfort with his/her spiritual discoveries. May Love and Light fill all his/her coming days. And, so it is.

Leader: (Taking up the bowl of water, blessing it.) Leader dips fingers into water and touches the baby's crown saying:

In the presence of and with the power of the Most High, and in the presence and Love of his/her parents and loving family, I name (christen) you, (Baby's full name.)

Leader dips fingers into water again and gently touches each shoulder, the throat, the heart, and the feet of the baby. Move the hand again to the crown saying:

From this time forward, (Baby's full name), you are blessed with the power of your name and all the spiritual qualities and resources you will need to fulfill God's purpose for your life. May God bless you and keep you, renew and protect you and may you always walk in beauty and balance upon this earth. May God awaken all your gifts to heal the world. (Optional to kiss the baby's forehead)

Leader: Blessing to all. *May the Holy Spirit guide and protect this child and all who have gathered to bless this new life. Welcome (Baby's full name) into your loving family and into your spiritual community. And, so it is.*

BLESSING OF THE FAMILY

Family is an important structure that binds us together in special ways. We belong to all kinds of families, our biological family, our extended family, the human family, and the family of all Creation. We even have an inner family of heart, mind and spirit. With the onset of technology, humanity is realizing that we are a global family. Family is a basic part of our lives and should be honored and blessed.

Many people believe that we choose our family members before we are born to help provide the challenges we want to resolve in this lifetime. Other people believe that we have no choice, that it is the choice of the Divine or fate. Whichever belief is held, family is still an important and crucial part of our lives. We are at our best in a "family."

This simple blessing ceremony can be performed with any kind of "family." The family members gather in a circle with the intention of sharing positive thoughts and feelings.

Supplies: A candle to light in the center of the circle, water in a small container.

Instructions: Form a circle holding hands which includes everyone in the family. (This can also be done around a table before a meal.) Invite the members to take a few moments of quiet to bring peace to the circle.

Opening

Leader: *We are a family of love, joy, and peace. Each family member is important and cherished. Without each person our family would not be complete. We honor all our family who have gone before us (The names of deceased relatives may be added here in remembrance) and all our family who will come after us. We learn important lessons from each member of our family.*

We are also a part of the greater family of the Divine (God). Each of us has an important part to play in the Divine Plan for humanity. It calls us to be the best that we can be, to treat each other with respect, and to honor the Divine within each of us.

We are so grateful to be a part of this family and a part of all our other families. We are a blessing to each other. Let us go around the circle and let our hearts speak a blessing about our family.

Bless the water and then the parents go to each child, taking a little water on the fingers and touching the top of the child's head, saying, "I bless you my child with love and peace." Each child goes to each parent, taking a little water on the fingers and touching the top of the parent's head, saying, "I bless you mother/father with love and peace."

Leader: *Thank you, O Divine Spirit, for our family and for all our blessings And, so it is.*

DEDICATION CEREMONY FOR BLENDING FAMILIES OR WELCOMING ADOPTED CHILDREN INTO A FAMILY

In modern times, many families are blended with children from one or both parents coming together to form a new family. Sometimes during the wedding ceremony of the parents, which is a spiritual ceremony, there is a dedication for the children, but most of the time the children are just thrown together and expected to become a family. This is an important time for the children as well as the parents and should be marked with a ceremony that speaks to the heart and soul of all the members of the new family.

Adopted children also need a spiritual ceremony to mark this important transitional time for them. Court room proceedings and parties are not enough for the tender souls of these children.

Instead of godparents, a family may name one, or two, Family Angels, who stand with the parents as advocates and supporters of the children. Family Angels are other adults the children may turn to when needed and should be chosen carefully. They are included in the ceremony.

It is a good idea to explain the purpose of the ceremony to the children, so they understand that they are special and are being welcomed into the new family.

Supplies: Candle to light to make the ceremony sacred; a gift for each of the children to be welcomed into the family held by the Family Angels until given to each child. (Examples of gifts for the children: engraved necklaces or bracelets, special figurines, family symbols.)

Instructions: This ceremony can be performed with only the children, the parents, and the Family Angels or other family members and friends can be invited. Light the candle and form a circle of attendees.

Leader: *Today we come together to celebrate the creation of a new family to be blessed by the Divine (God). Will (Names of children and parents) please come forward and take hands?*

(Father's name) do you promise to take care of (children's names), to love them, and to respect and honor each one as a member of your new family? (I do). *(Mother's name) do you promise to take care of (children's names), to love them, and to respect and honor each one as a member of your new family?* (I do).

(Children's names) do you promise to do your best to be a part of this family, to make it strong, and to listen to, care for, and support your parents and the other children? (We do)

Will all of you in this new family promise to love one another, to work together, to play and laugh together, and to be always mindful that your family is a family of God? (We will.)

Family Angels, will you promise to love and support, nurture and guide, this new family, and to support the spiritual life of each member? (We do)

(To the other people gathered) *As the greater family for (Names of family members), will you promise to support and love this new family and to do everything you can to help them?* (We will)

What gifts do you bring to seal this new family with love? (Gifts are handed to the parents to be given to each child)

O Great Spirit, Guardian of all Families, we pray that this new family will learn and grow together building the bond of love between them and with You. We ask that you watch over them, care for and provide for them. Bless each of these parents and each of these children with Your love and grace. In Your Holy Name, we pray. Amen. (And, so it is.)

Please join hands with your Family Angels. *Forasmuch as (Names of parents and children) have pledged and promised to love one another and God, to laugh and play and grow together, we now declare that they are a true family dedicated in love. May God bless you and keep you and may God ever watch over you and bring you and your new family peace.*

Notes: If the family is welcoming an adopted child, the ceremony can easily be changed.

Ceremonies and Blessings for Life Changes

CEREMONIES AND BLESSINGS FOR LIFE CHANGES

Each life change is an opportunity for renewal of heart, mind and spirit. Some life changes come unexpectedly while others come as planned. Life changes mark the crossroads of our lives and an opportunity to choose a different way. Life changes are also those markers that help us remember we are no longer the person we used to be but the new person we are becoming. Our first life change comes when we leave the comfort of the womb to push out into a new world. The last life change comes when we leave the old physical body behind and resume our true body of light.

Girls who have been honored in the Moonflower Ceremony and boys who have been honored in the Way of the Wolf Ceremony tell us that these ceremonies have made a great difference in their lives. Elders also report feeling honored with the Wise Woman and Wise Man ceremonies marking their life change of moving into Elderhood.

MOONFLOWER CEREMONY FOR GIRLS
(Based on traditional cultural ceremonies)

This ceremony marks a young woman's transition from girlhood to womanhood. It is celebrated as close to her first moon cycle as possible. It is a time for all women to honor the Holy Goddess, the Holy Mother within. It is the time to remember a woman's special connection to her sisters and to Mother Earth. **ONLY WOMEN AND GIRLS ARE ALLOWED TO PARTICIPATE IN THIS CEREMONY.** Four women are selected to represent the Four Directions before the ceremony begins and sit in their direction within the circle.

Supplies: Five copies of the ceremony, one for the Leader and one each for the Four Directions; smudging supplies, if desired; scarf to use as a blindfold; flower wreath with red flowers and red ribbons for the young woman; altar cloth placed on ground or on a small table in the center of the circle; chairs for the participants or they may sit on the ground; a candle lighter and four votive candles, and objects for the Four Directions; four-stemmed flowers as offerings to the women of the Four Directions ball of red yarn and scissors; anointing oil or olive oil; heart-shaped locket from the gathering of Sisters.

East: Green votive candle, small bunch of flowers; symbol of a bird
South: Blue votive candle, seashell and symbol of a dolphin
West: Red votive candle, autumn leaves and symbol of a horse
North: White votive candle, cornmeal in a small container, symbol of a bear

Instructions: Prior to the ceremony any woman who wishes to smudge herself may do so. A circle is set up out in nature, if possible, with the altar in the center. The Moonflower maiden is dressed in a simple skirt and top with her hair hanging down. Outside the circle, all the participants hug her goodbye symbolizing her departure from childhood. She is then blindfolded with the scarf to symbolize the unknown future and led by a circuitous route to her place of honor in the circle. The other women form a line behind her and spiral dance to the circle and take their places. The maiden remains standing in front of her chair with the blindfold on. Her mother and grandmother or older sister stand on each side.

Opening

Leader: We offer this prayer to the Four Directions. *Be with us now Spirits of the East, South, West, and North, as we celebrate this young woman's transition from maiden to woman. Be with us as we reconnect with the Holy Mother and with each other and be with (name) as she takes this sacred step. With this ceremony we honor the Holy Mother of all Life.*

The grandmother or older sister removes the blindfold and the mother of the Maiden places the wreath of flowers on her head, kisses her on the cheek, and everyone is seated.

Leader: (Name), be welcome now into the Circle of Power of the Goddess. Let us all enter into a few moments of silence by closing our eyes and taking four deep breaths to get centered. Let each feel the inner power rising to fill our whole being so that we may be fully present here for our new sister (Name).

Let us pray: *Holy Mother of All Life, we come today to this place and to this time to honor you through the blessing of (Name). We acknowledge your presence as Mother Earth, from whence all life springs forth. We honor your presence as the Moon Goddess who controls our bodies and our emotions in the cycle of life. We honor your power through our ability to create new life in your holy name. We feel your eternal love that defines us with feminine joy and blessings of motherhood. We ask that you be present with (Name) as she leaves her childhood behind and enters into her days of womanhood. We ask your blessings on each of the women gathered here in your name. And, so it is.*

Blessings of the Four Directions

Leader: Let each woman representing the Four Directions come forward now and light the candle of their Direction and read the blessings for (Name).

EAST (Green): *I am the Woman of the East. I ask the Wisdom of the East to be present with (Name) to bless her with the spirits of Air, of spring and the energy of the rising sun. I bring flower blossoms to represent spring and a Bird to represent the spirits of the Air. I light the green candle.* (Light candle) *I ask that (Name) be blessed with the beauty of new beginnings. May her new beginning as a woman deepen her connection to her inner self, to the intuition of the Goddess within, and to the sensations of the world outside. May the spirit of the Bird renew her special connection to the spirit of the East and help her enter womanhood with grace and joy. I thank you, Wisdom of the East.* (Maiden rises and offers a flower to the Woman of the East and thanks her for her teachings.)

SOUTH (Blue): *I am the Woman of the South. I ask that the Wisdom of the South be present with (Name), to bless her with the spirits of water, of summer and the energy of the noonday sun. I bring a seashell to represent summer and a Dolphin to represent the spirits of the Water. I light the blue candle.* (Light candle). *I ask that (Name) be blessed by keeping her childlike wonder, the qualities of spontaneity and fun. May the spirit of the Dolphin watch over her and bless her as she emerges from childhood to womanhood. May she always be aware of her special connection to the spirit of the South as she grows in feminine energy. I thank you, Spirit of the South.* (Maiden rises and offers a flower to the Woman of the South and thanks her for her teachings.)

WEST (Red): *I am the Woman of the West. I ask the Wisdom of the West be present with (Name), to bless her with the spirits of Fire, of autumn, and the energy of the setting sun. I bring colorful leaves to represent fall and a Horse to represent the spirits of Fire. I light the red candle.* (Light candle) *I ask that (Name) be blessed with the passion of the West and the ability* to *develop strong and loving relationships. May she always remember the love of her family. May the spirit of the Horse help her to be strong, loving and loyal. Give her the freedom to be herself. May she always be aware of her special connection to the spirit of the West as she grows into the best person she can be. I thank you, Wisdom of the West.* (Maiden rises and offers a flower to the Woman of the West and thanks her for her teachings.)

NORTH (White): *I am the Woman of the North. I ask the Wisdom of the North to be present with (Name), the spirits of Earth, of winter, and the darkness of the night, the luminosity of the moon and inner strength. I bring cornmeal, the gift from the Goddess, and a Bear. I light the white candle.* (Light candle) *I ask that (Name) be blessed with the qualities of winter, the ability to be quiet and to listen to her inner spirit. May she know the beauty of waiting for the fullness of ideas and desires. May the spirit of the Bear strengthen and protect her and teach her the value of patience and waiting for the proper time. I thank you Wisdom of the North.* (Maiden rises and offers a flower to the Woman of the North and thanks her for her teachings.)

Leader: Thank you, Women of the Four Directions for your blessings for (Name).

Ritual of Connection

Leader: We come together in sisterhood with all women and all the females in all creation. Today we reaffirm our connections with each other and all the women who have gone before us and honor our uniqueness and creativity by spinning the web of life. (Take ball of red yarn in one hand) I will pass around this red yarn symbolizing our moon cycles that connects all women in sisterhood. Wrap your wrist with a loop of yarn and recite your mother's first name. Then wrap another loop reciting her mother's name, going back as far as you know. Then pass the yarn to the next person or to the person across the circle. As the names of our mother ancestors are spoken, let us honor and remember each soul who has brought us to this place and time. (Name) will be last one to recite her mothers' names. When all of the names have been recited and remembered and we are all connected through time and space, we will take a few moments to send loving energy to all these women who have come before us. (Leader begins: I am (Name) the daughter of (Name) who is the daughter of (Name)…)

When all women have wrapped the yarn around their wrists and recited their mothers' names and sent the loving energy to their ancestors, the scissors are passed around.

Leader: Cut off enough yarn to tie a knot and secure your arm bracelet. Wear this bracelet for the rest of the day or longer if you choose. As you cut your bracelet, please share a story about (Name) or remind her of some positive quality that she can take into womanhood.

Self-Blessing Ritual of the Goddess

Leader: As we have blessed and honored our female ancestors, our mothers and our grandmothers, and blessed (Name), we will now bless the Goddess within by blessing our female bodies. I will be using anointing oil to bless (Name). You are welcome to use some oil for your blessing. Gently and lovingly touch the different parts of your body in this blessing of the Goddess within. (Pass oil around)

Bless me Mother,
Bless my eyes to behold only beauty around me,
Bless my nose to smell the sweet essence of life,
Bless my lips to speak only good and healing words,
Bless my ears to hear the cry of those in need,
Bless my breasts, that I may comfort and sustain life,
Bless my womb that my creativity may grow strong and flourish,
Bless my source of creation, that brings forth life for good,
Bless my hands to do your sacred work,
Bless my feet to walk on the straight path of honor,
Bless my heart to know your wisdom.
Thank you, Holy Mother, for being with me always. Your Love and Light sustain and protect me.
Thank you for the abundant blessings of my life.
Bless me, Mother, for I am your sacred child and your holy woman. (Bring hands to prayer position)

Conclusion

Leader: (Name), we celebrate you this day and this exciting time of your life as you move from the sacred years of maidenhood into the holy years of womanhood. You now experience balance and appreciation for your mind, your heart, your soul, and your body, which now moves in harmony with the moon. Allow your awareness to blossom in every way, expressing the perfect, whole, powerful beauty of being a woman in your chosen time. Know that you are, through us, your Sisters, connected to the beginning, to the Goddess, the Source of Life. She lives as you live, sees as you see, loves as you love, guides, protects and holds you in her heart. She knows your name and who you are. Keep the Goddess always in your heart. To remind you that the Goddess is always in your heart, your Sisters have a gift for you. (Mother or relative fastens locket around her neck.)

Hear now the words of Wisdom from your new Sisters. (Any woman may speak and give her words of wisdom).

Leader: To close our ceremony, will the Women of the Four Directions come forward as I read the closing prayers and blow out their candles.

As the spirits of the North leave us, please impart your solitude and peacefulness to us and to (Name) as she prepares for the challenges ahead.

As the spirits of the West leave us, we ask your energy and creativity to inspire us and (Name) as she begins a new way of living and being.

As the spirits of the South leave us, may (Name) remember to trust the innocent spirit with her as we remember to trust our own innocent spirit.

As the spirits of the East leave us, let (Name) soar upon them to new beginnings trusting her intuition to guide her and may we also be guided.

We thank the Spirits of the Four Directions as representatives of the Holy Mother for bringing us together and for blessing our circle. We release them now with gratitude and deep appreciation. Let us stand and form a circle around (Name). May we find our own lives blessed as we have blessed (Name) this day and may the connection of Sisterhood strengthen as we all grow into the sacred women we are meant to be. Amen. And, so it is.

Women hug (Name) symbolizing her acceptance into the greater Sisterhood. Gifts are presented, and refreshments are served.

WAY OF THE WOLF CEREMONY FOR BOYS

In our society boys lack clear markers for the time when they become men. It is said in Western countries that "25 is the new 15" implying that young men are expected to stay boys until they reach their mid-twenties. In traditional societies coming of age ceremonies are held for boys between the ages of 13 and 15 depending on the culture. It is the time when a boy steps into his responsibilities as a man, to take his rightful place in the society, and to use his gifts and talents to make a difference in the world.

This ceremony can be performed for a boy from age 13-15. It is a good time to make a ceremony for boys moving from middle school into high school to help prepare them for the added responsibilities and pressures of growing faster into manhood. **ONLY MEN AND BOYS ARE**

ALLOWED TO BE A PART OF THIS CEREMONY. An outdoor setting is best – in a park or in the woods.

The boy may be given a new name, which is whispered to him for the first time by his father or other male family representative at the end of the ceremony. It can also be engraved on a bracelet.

Supplies: Five copies of the ceremony, one for the Leader and one each for the Four Directions; smudging supplies, if desired; scarf to use as a blindfold; symbols of the Five Elements of Fire (pyramid crystal), Water (seashell), Earth (stone), Air (Feather), and Metal (flint); statue of a wolf to be given to the boy after the ceremony; circular or small blanket for boy to sit on; brown face paint. Gift – ID bracelet, small knife, etc. Two small bowls, one filled with tobacco and one filled with cornmeal. Small colored cloths for each of the Four Directions: red-East; green-South; black-West; white-North. Drums may also be a part of this ceremony.

Instructions: Set the blanket in the center of the circle for the boy. Chairs may be set around the circle for men who cannot sit on the ground. Appoint four men to represent the Four Directions, who will offer the Teachings of the Directions to the boy, and a Leader who will help the boy through the ceremony. Another man is needed to present the different items used in the ceremony. The men of the Four Directions will sit in their direction

Place the items used in the ceremony on a red cloth in the East – the direction of new beginnings. When all participants have gathered, and the ceremony set up, the sage is lit and all who desire may smudge themselves. Smudge the boy last and the men tell him goodbye and/or shake his hand. He is then blindfolded and led around the outside of the circle in a random manner by the Leader and the men of the Four Directions. This represents his path through childhood being blind to the world of the Warrior. All others may enter the circle and begin drumming.

The Leader meets the boy in the East and leads him around the circle clockwise, returning to the East and then to the Center of the circle and removes the blindfold. The drumming ceases. All stand for the prayers to the Four Directions, then the boy sits down on the blanket.

The teachings are given as the boy moves around the circle. When the teachings are over, he returns to sit in the center for the Five Elements ritual. The boy's father or grandfather or nearest male relative brings the bowl of face paint for the next teaching.

Opening

Leader: We are gathered here today, fathers, grandfathers, uncles, cousins and friends of (Name) to celebrate his first step on becoming a Warrior through the Way of the Wolf. (Name) has the support of the men in his family, and in his community, who are here for him, to guide and support him on this important journey.

Let us pray: *Great Spirit, whose voice we hear in the winds and whose breath gives life to all creation, we come to you with clean hands and straight eyes. We ask for your strength and wisdom as this young Wolf begins his journey to manhood. Make his way straight so that he may respect all of your creation and learn to live in right relationship with all things. Give him a gentle heart, a keen mind, and strength to take his place as a Warrior to protect the people. Aho.*

Prayers to the Four Directions

All stand and face East: *Be with us Grandfather Spirit of the East, the place of new beginnings. Guide (Name) as he learns to walk boldly into his new beginnings. Aho.*

Face South: *Be with us Grandfather Spirit of the South, the place of lessons and knowledge. Teach (Name) what it is to be a Warrior and to walk the path of his life in balance. Aho.*

Face West: *Be with us Grandfather Spirit of the West, the place where we put our knowledge into practice to care for others and for Mother Earth and all her children. Show (Name) the way of the animals and the birds. Aho.*

Face North: *Be with us Grandfather Spirit of the North, the quiet place of reflection. Lead (Name) into the wisdom of the silence and to know when it is right to be still and to listen to the voice of the Creator. Aho.*

Face Center: *Be with us Grandfather Sky, home of our ancestors and our Elders. Be with (Name) as he embraces the wisdom of all the Men who have gone before him. Aho.*

Be with us Grandmother Earth, nurturer of all life. Be with (Name) as he learns gentleness and the power of walking in beauty upon your land. Aho.

Leader: We gather in this Circle of Power to welcome (Name) into the Circle of Warriors and Elders as he leaves behind his childhood to walk in the ways of men. We, who are his brothers, bring him into this Circle to learn of the things of men, of how to walk in the world with courage, truth, and balance and become a true Warrior of Peace.

Teaching of the Medicine Wheel

Leader: This circle that we have created represents the sacred Medicine Wheel of Life. Each person stands in the center with the Creator, in relationship to everything else in the world. The Medicine Wheel is also a mirror reflecting back to our eyes what we believe. Our Teachers tell us that all things within this Medicine Wheel know of their Harmony with every other thing and know how to give-away one to the other, except man. Of all the creatures in the Universe, it is man alone who does not begin his life with the knowledge of this Great Harmony. He must learn to give away. All the things in the Medicine Wheel of Life have spirit and life, but it is only man who is the chooser, the determiner. We can be made whole only through learning about our place in the Great Harmony. We find this place through living with all our relations. We find this place by discovering who we are, how we perceive ourselves and others, and finding harmonious relationship with the world around us. This is the teaching of the Medicine Wheel. To gain wisdom as a man, we must look at the world from all the directions. Each event in a man's life begins in the East.

(Name), take up your blanket and seat yourself in front of the Grandfather of the East, offer him tobacco, and say *"Grandfather, please teach me of the wisdom of the East."* The Grandfather receives the tobacco and places it on the yellow cloth.

Grandfather of the East: The East is the place of beginning in the Golden Dawn. The power color of the East is golden yellow as the rising sun. This is the place of illumination. We all have our beginning in the dawn of life. The animal of the East is the Eagle who soars upon the wind rising higher and higher in the sky. With his keen eyes he can see clearly. He can see truth and hope. You must see clearly before you take off to soar with the Eagle. Look at things carefully before you take the first step, so you will know the truth. (Name), may you find courage in the East to walk the circle of your life with honesty and dignity. These are the teachings of the East.

Boy says, *"Thank you Grandfather of the East for this teaching."* He gives him a pinch of cornmeal and the Grandfather places it on the cloth next to the tabacco.

He rises and takes his blanket and moves clockwise to the South sitting in front of the Grandfather of the South. He offers him tobacco and asks, *"Grandfather, please teach me of the wisdom of the South."* The Grandfather receives the tobacco and places it on the green cloth.

Grandfather of the South: The South is the place of learning and gaining knowledge. The power color of the South is Green, the color of growth. This the direction you are in as you move from childhood to manhood, from Explorer to Warrior. The animal of the South is the Wolf, who teaches us about working together. The Wolf remembers to honor and trust his heart and that good decisions come from the heart. He wanders far and discovers the world outside his den. The South teaches about compassion for our relations that live upon our Great Mother. To know your place in the world is to recognize your own self-worth for you always stand strong with Creator. (Name), may you walk your path with joy and love for yourself and for all Creation. Grow with knowledge and nurture yourself. These are the teachings of the South.

Boy says, *"Thank you, Grandfather of the South for this teaching."* He gives him a pinch of cornmeal and the Grandfather places it on the cloth next to the tabacco.

He takes his blanket and moves clockwise to the West sitting in front of the Grandfather of the West. He offers him tobacco and asks, *"Grandfather, please teach me of the wisdom of the West."* The Grandfather receives the tobacco and places it on the black cloth.

Grandfather of the West: The West is the place where all you have learned and experienced is put into practice. Your decisions are now based on both heart and mind to benefit all. The power color of the West is black which represents the unknown that we must learn to experience with courage and bravery. It is also the color of infinite possibilities. The animal of the West is the Brown Bear, who is Keeper of all the Medicines, who knows how to heal. The bear brings healing to all the people. The Bear knows when it is time to rest and when it is time to act. This is the way of balance. The West teaches that balance is powerful – the balance between heart, mind, and spirit. When you are in balance you know your place in this world. (Name), may you walk in beauty and balance with light, joy and the awareness of your spirit nature. These are the teachings of the West.

Boy says, *"Thank you, Grandfather of the West for this teaching."* He gives him a pinch of cornmeal which the Grandfather places on the cloth next to the tabacco.

He takes his blanket and moves clockwise to the North sitting in front of the Grandfather of the North. He offers him tobacco and asks, *"Grandfather, please teach me of the Wisdom of the North."* The Grandfather receives the tobacco and places it on the white cloth.

Grandfather of the North: The North is the direction of reflection and quiet. In the North we listen to Creator, we listen to the world, and we listen to our own spirit. The North shows us what we have to release that no longer serves us. The animal of the North is the sacred White Buffalo symbolizing spiritual wisdom. The White Buffalo helps us make wise choices based on Spirit. The North provides serenity and comfort. When it is our time to pass to the next hunting grounds, the North takes us peacefully if we have a pure heart. (Name), may you find wisdom, truth, and purity of heart as you walk your path of life. These are the teachings of the North.

Boy says, *"Thank you Grandfather of the North for this teaching."* He gives him a pinch of cornmeal which the Grandfather places next to the tobacco.

The Boy takes his blanket and moves back to sit in the center of the circle.

Leader: Every man's life is made of the Five Elements. As these elements are presented to you, your father will make the mark on your face signifying you have now integrated the teachings of the elements into your spirit. (Helper brings the elements and hands each to the boy in turn.)

The Element of Water – *You were born of water, the symbol of life. As water moves through its cycle, you too move through your cycle of life. Learn to ebb and flow like the water.* (Hand the element of water to the boy. The first mark is placed vertically on his forehead.)

The Element of Earth – *You live on this earth, the symbol of our physical being. It is from the earth that we are formed and on the earth that we live. Know that this earth form is sacred.* (Hand the element of earth to the boy. The second mark is placed horizontally on his right cheek.)

The Element of Fire – *You are filled with fire that shapes and molds us from the inside out. Fire is the symbol of transformation. When you light the flame, go deep within it to that point of transformation.* (Hand the element of fire to the boy. The third mark is placed horizontally on his left cheek.)

The Element of Air – *You cannot live without air. Air is the symbol of higher consciousness, of holy thought, of growth in non-ordinary dimensions. With every breath you take, remember to uplift heart and mind to the sacred.* (Hand the element of Air to the boy and the fourth mark is made vertically on his chin.)

The Element of Metal – *You have the power to make changes and metal is the symbol of what we make of ourselves. It is the catalyst for change. As you were given this pure form of metal, mold it and shape it wisely as you will mold and shape your life.* (Hand the element of Metal to the boy and the final mark is made vertically down his nose.)

Leader: (Name), please rise. You have been welcomed into the Great Circle of the Warriors, you have received the teachings of the Medicine Wheel and the teachings of the Four Directions, and you have honored the Five Elements of life, you are now ready to begin your journey as a man, a Warrior. Let your first steps as a man be as sacred as your last steps. Receive this gift from these Warriors to remind you that today you are a man. (Present gift to the new Warrior).

Leader: Today, you also receive your new spiritual name of _____. Take the hand of your father as an equal and lead us around the circle as you begin the first part of your journey connected to all the men in your family and all men in the Great Circle of Life.

The new Warrior takes his father's hand, the drumming begins and dancing (toe-heel, step, toe-heel), he leads all the men around the circle one time and out the East to his new beginning. (Refreshments may be served)

WISE WOMAN CEREMONY

There are few ceremonies that mark a woman's transition to becoming a Wise Woman or Grandmother. This is a very important time for a woman. Her days raising children have come to an end and she is learning to relate to her adult children in a different way. She is finally coming into her own power and, if she is supported with love and respect, she will become the healer she was meant to be. Only a woman can determine when she is ready for this important ceremony. **THIS IS A CEREMONY FOR WOMEN AND GIRLS ONLY. WOMEN FRIENDS AND FAMILY MEMBERS ARE ESPECIALLY INVITED TO THIS CEREMONY**

Supplies: Ceremonial gifts – crystal, bouquet of herbs wrapped with a blue ribbon, symbol of the moon, white flower corsage made with artificial flowers; basket with clear stones; shawl; other gifts brought for the new Wise Woman, circle of chairs, sage for smudging, optional. (Other Wise Women attending are invited to wear their Shawls to this ceremony.)

Instructions: Create a circle of chairs with the Wise Woman's chair in the North facing south. Put the basket of clear stones next to it. Have a clear space to create the birthing bridge. Appoint four Wise Women to represent the Grandmothers of the Four Directions during the ceremony. (Have sage ready for smudging for those who desire to be cleansed before the ceremony)

Opening

Leader: Life is a Great Circle. (Name) has now moved into the North of her journey. We gather today to celebrate this special time in her life as she becomes the Wise Woman, the Healer. Women are the birthers of life and we begin our Circle by walking through the birthing bridge, the birth canal, into our rightful place as we chant. Two women form a bridge by touching their hands together overhead. The next two women walk under the bridge and form the next section. As more women go through the bridge, they began to form the Circle. (Name) and I will be the last two women to enter. When the last two women go through the birthing bridge, the first two women join hands and walk back through the birthing bridge single file, bringing the other women with them, continuing on to form a circle as they emerge. When the circle is complete, all stand in silence for a moment breathing in the sacredness of the moment.

All the Women say together as they form the Birthing Bridge: *We are women, we are holy. We are women, we are sacred. We are women, we give birth to life.*

Leader: We are the holy, sacred women. Let us pray. *Mother God, we give thanks for your presence in our lives. We give thanks for this gathering of your daughters, Maidens, Mothers and Wise Women. We ask your blessings on (Name), who is newly come to her Wise Woman way. Teach her and guide her in the paths of healing as she comes into her perfect time. May she always walk in your Wisdom. So, mote it be.*

This is a time of celebration of the attainment of the age of wisdom in a woman's life and we celebrate with our Sister (Name). She has already gone through the changes in body, mind, heart and spirit to reach her potential as healer. Our patriarchal society does not recognize women of this age as wise and powerful and important. Usually they are defined by their physiological functions and when those functions wane, they are considered to be old, useless and dysfunctional. But Women of Wisdom know the Truth. They are forever young, essential and aware of their rightful place as wise Healers and Counselors in the Great Circle of Life.

In celebrating the Wise Woman, we honor bodily changes as a beginning of a new freedom. We honor changing relationships as noble and realize change is the Divine Plan. We honor the healing gifts we bring to this time of life. We honor our experiences as women, respecting all our stories of survival and growth. And we honor the Divine Mother who brings us into the light of our own being. Today we honor our new Wise Woman – (Name).

The Circles of Life

Leader: We begin our ceremony with the Circles of Life. This outer Circle in which we stand symbolizes our first decade of life. Each of us in turn, using just a word or two, will name something we want to remember about our first decade. When the circle is completed, women who have reached the next decade will take one step forward, creating the next circle and saying what they wish to remember about the 2nd decade of life. We will continue until the last decade represented in the group is completed. You may just step forward without saying anything or you may say "I survived," as you think about your own life. When we reach the 6th or 7th decade our new Wise Woman will step into the center of the circle. All the women who have attained 60 years of age will also step into the center of the circle. Everyone else may return to the outer circle and sit down.

Honoring the Grandmothers of the Four Directions

Leader: We honor the Four Directions and the Grandmothers in Spirit in this inner Circle. Will our oldest Wise Woman please do the honors with this bowl of water? Please stand while we honor the Grandmothers in Spirit. (Oldest Wise Woman presents the bowl of water to each of the Four Directions, Father Sky and Mother Earth inviting them to be with the Circle.)

(Name), you have moved around the Great Wheel of Life from East to West, from South to North, and it is here in the North that you now reside. It is a place of power and a place of healing. It is a place of deep contemplation and wisdom. This is your rightful place now. Claim it by sitting in the chair of the north. You may all be seated.

Leader: Takes the bowl of water and anoints the honored Wise Woman. *Every woman should be blessed and know she is blessed as a daughter of the Great Mother, the Holy Goddess. I bless you now, (Name), with this holy water, the water of your life and ours.* (Leader dips fingers into water and places the hand on the top of the head and sends a silent blessing for [Name]).

The Blessing Gifts

Leader: As (Name) is honored in this ceremony today, we also honor our other Wise Women. Will all the Wise Women please stand in place for this part of the ceremony? As each of the Grandmothers of the Four Directions gives (Name) her Wise Woman gifts, she will pass each gift around the Circle to all the Wise Women. As the Wise Women receives the gift in her hand, receive the blessings of the gift for yourself and add your own before passing it on around the Circle back to the Grandmother of the Four Directions to present the blessed gift to (Name).

Grandmother of the East, please step forward with your gift for (Name). *This gift from the east is a crystal to remind you that the sun always rises in this place of new beginnings. Each day this crystal will awaken you to your own power of healing. Be blessed by the Grandmother of the East.* (Hand gift to [Name}, who passes it to the first Wise Woman in the Circle, who blesses it and passes it on. When the last Wise Woman hands it back, the Grandmother presents it to [Name] and returns to her seat.)

Grandmother of the South, please step forward with your gift for (Name) *This gift from the South is a bouquet of herbs to remind you that you still have room to grow. The gift of herbs is to help you with your healing of others. Learn the way of herbs and be blessed by the Grandmother of the South.* (Gift of herbs is passed around, blessed, and presented to [Name].)

Grandmother of the West, please step forward with your gift for (Name) *This gift from the West is a symbol of the Moon, for when you become a Wise Woman you are no longer tied to the pull of the Moon but instead can use the power of the Moon in your healing work. Be blessed by the moon and the Grandmother of the West.* (Moon gift symbol is passed around, blessed, and presented to [Name].)

Grandmother of the North, please step forward with your gift for (Name). *This gift from the North is a white corsage made of flowers that never fade. They are held in the white of the North to remind you that your Source is always there ready to come forward to help with your healing service. Be blessed by these flowers and the Northern Grandmother.* (Corsage is passed is passed around, blessed, and pinned on [Name].)

The Blessings of the Wise Women

Each Wise Woman may now come forward one at a time to take (Name's) hand in turn and give her a blessing, a word of advice, or a word of congratulations as she joins her Sisters in Healing. As she receives her blessing, she will hand each of you a gift of a crystal stone symbolizing her gratitude for participating in this Wise Woman ceremony with her.

Pledge

Leader: (Name) please stand now and place your hands over your heart to make your pledge. *Do you accept whole-heartedly your role as Wise Woman and the Healer Who Knows? Do you pledge yourself to be of service, to listen with compassion, and speak the wisdom from your heart? Do you dedicate the rest of your life to this healing work, always learning, growing, and sharing?* Then answer, *"I do with all my heart, mind and spirit."*

Presentation of the Shawl*

Leader: As a symbol of your new status, we present you with this shawl, weaving together the strands of your life to wrap you in warmth and comfort when times are hard, and to wear with dignity and honor as you claim your Wise Woman place.* We want you to know that this community of women supports you in your journey forward, that we praise and bless you. We are so grateful that we will learn from you and feel your healing power. To all our Wise Women honored today, we support you, praise and bless you. We continue to learn from you and feel your healing power. You are the healers of this community and we are so grateful for each and every one of you. Blessings on all our Wise Women.

Gifts from the Sisterhood

You may come forward and present your gifts to our new Wise Woman with your blessings.

Prayer of Blessings

Leader: Each woman is invited now to come forward to bless (Name), our new Wise Woman. We will place our hands on (Name) for the closing prayer as the Goddess blesses her through us.

Thank you, Divine Mother, for bringing (Name) to this special place in her life and for bringing all our Wise Women to their special places. We thank the Grandmothers of the Four Directions for being here with us in this ceremony and release them now. We thank all the women here today and bless each one on their journey to healing and power. We are Sisters to each other and to all other women. So, mote it be.

Closing Circle

Leader: Let us join in the women's handhold** and sing, *"We are weaving peace together. We are weaving peace together. We are weaving peace together, Daughters of the Earth…Sisters of the Light… Women of the Stars." (Sung to "We are Climbing Jacob's Ladder).*

Notes: *The Shawl may be one the new Wise Woman already has that has been re-blessed or a new one. The shawl presentation is optional.

**The women's handhold for the Closing Circle is the basket hold. Each woman stands with arms held down to the sides diagonally in front of the person standing beside her on each side. She takes the hands of the second person standing next to her in the circle forming a basket-weave handhold.

WISE MAN CEREMONY

Men are not honored enough for their spiritual achievements of becoming who they truly are as representatives of the divine masculine power and energy of the Universe. This ceremony blesses a man who is moving from a Sacred Warrior to his highest role as Shaman, Wise Man, in the community. It makes this a sacred time as he matures into the role of Healer and Wise Counselor for the younger men. They need the wisdom gained from his life experiences and they need his guidance to help them along the journey. Becoming a Grandfather means more than just having grandchildren. It is symbolic of being a channel for the spiritual wisdom that comes from the masculine aspect of God: to be strong yet stand in peace; to use the mind to see a broader perspective; to transform passion into compassion.

This is the time of true power recognized without words and if a man is supported with love and respect, he will become the Healer he was meant to be. Only a man can determine when he is ready for this important ceremony. **THIS IS A CEREMONY FOR MEN AND BOYS ONLY. MALE FRIENDS AND FAMILY MEMBERS ARE ESPECIALLY INVITED TO ATTEND THIS CEREMONY.**

Supplies: Drum, blue face paint in a bowl, paper towels, gifts representing the Five Elements, other gifts for the new Wise Man, (a new belt buckle, book, knife) circle of chairs, basket of colored stones. (Sage for smudging, optional)

Instructions: Create a circle of chairs with the Wise Man's chair in the North facing south. Put the basket of colored stones next to it. Have a clear space to create the Trials of Life. Appoint five men to represent the Five Elements during the ceremony. (Have sage ready for smudging for those who desire to be cleansed before the ceremony)

Opening

Leader: We are gathered today to celebrate and acknowledge (Name) as he takes his place as a Wise Man, a Shaman, of our community. After this ceremony he will no longer be a Sacred Warrior but claim his rightful place as Healer and Wise Counselor. This is the time to release the struggles of youth, to let go of striving and fighting, and embrace the peace of becoming. It is the time to fully accept your unique wisdom and return to the great Circle of Life all that you have learned, all that you have experienced, and all that you have become. You are now the Healer Who Knows. With this ceremony we also honor all Wise Men in our community and in the world.

The Trials of Life

Leader: We begin by leading (Name) through the Trials of Life symbolizing the trials of linear time in the physical world and the trials of the spiritual world in circular time, and the connections of both in our lives. Please form two lines facing each other and make a bridge of arms. (Name) will go slowly under the bridge with the last two people following him in single file and on the other side, form a circle. (Name) then weaves in and out of the circle between the men. If anyone makes it difficult to get through for a moment, it symbolizes that not all challenges have been easy. (Drumming accompanies this part of the ceremony.)

(Name), you are called to step forward and confirm your decision to become a Wise Man. Come forward now and stand before your peers and in their presence, accept your new role in the community as that of the Healer Who Knows. (Lead new Wise Man into the circle of chairs to the seat in the North and everyone follows and stands in front of the chairs.)

Let us pray: *O, Great Spirit, be with us now as we affirm this man in his new role as Healer and Counselor. We call on all our Spirit Guides, Angels, Masters and Teachers to be with us and with him. We call on the ancestors, the Grandfathers of the Four Directions, and the Spirits of the Five Elements to be with us for this ceremony of transformation. Make sacred this time in his life and bring him wisdom, power, and love to fulfill his purpose on Earth. Bless him and guide him in all his ways as you bless him each of us. And, so it is.* (Be seated)

Honoring the Grandfathers of the Four Directions

Leader: (Name), you have come a long way from the hurts of childhood, from the terrors of war, from broken relationships. You have come a long way into joy, love and peace. Now is the time to step into your own healing and by doing so, you will help others heal. You will become the Healer Who Knows.

Everyone please stand and face the East. *Grandfather of the East, be with us now as (Name) stands on the verge of his new life as Healer and Wise Counselor. Show him that the ending of one life is always the beginning of a new life. Aho.*

Turn South. *Grandfather of the South, be with us now as (Name) learns what it is to be more than he was. Teach him the ways of the Healer and how to serve others with a new heart. Aho.*

Turn West. *Grandfather of the West, be with us now as (Name) transforms his life experience into wisdom to share with the greater family of life. Help him to know that wisdom sees the bigger picture of life so he may share with heart and mind. Aho.*

Turn North. *Grandfather of the North, be with us now as (Name) realizes the power of peace and calmness. Sit with him in the serenity of the winter of his life, sure of the power of resting in the stillness where all challenges and all solutions are frozen in time. Help him recognize and share the path of beauty and peace. Aho.*

Face center. *Grandfather Sky, be with us now as (Name) brings a new understanding of what it means to integrate the Explorer, Sacred Warrior, and Wise Man into the best expression of Your sacred words. Aho.*

Face downward. *Grandmother Earth, be with us now as (Name) becomes more rooted in your loving support to walk upon this land with dignity. Aho.*

The Circle may now be seated.

Honoring by the Five Elements

Leader: We are made of the stars as all of creation is made of the sacred cosmic dust. Within the cosmos are the Five Elements of transformative energy. To bring balance to our lives we honor all the elements. The Five Elements are Fire, Water, Earth, Air, and Metal. Each element flows into and out of our lives as we walk the path of our journey. As you hold in your hand each of these elements gifted to you, remember they are a part of you as you are a part of the stars.

Each representative of the Five Elements will now come forward, hand you the gift of their element and place a painted mark on your face to represent the balance of the five in the spiritual world.

The Element of Water – *You were born of water, the symbol of life. As water moves through its cycle, you too move through your cycle of life. Learn the balance of ebbing and flowing like the water so you may teach us harmony. Thank you, Spirit of Water, for your gifts.* (Representative of Water hands (Name) the symbol of water and paints a vertical mark on his forehead.)

The Element of Earth – *You live on this earth, the symbol of our physical being. It is from the earth that we are formed and on the earth that we live. Know that this earth form is sacred as the heavens are sacred. Thank you, Spirit of Earth, for your gifts.* (Representative of Earth hands (Name) the symbol of earth and paints a horizontal mark on his right cheek.)

The Element of Fire – *You are animated by fire. Fire shapes and molds us from the inside out. Fire is the symbol of transformation. When you light the flame, go deep within it to that point of transformation. Thank you, Spirit of Fire, for your gifts.* (Representative of Fire hands (Name) the symbol of fire and paints a horizontal mark on his left cheek.)

The Element of Air - *Without air you could not live. Air is the symbol of higher consciousness, of holy thought, of growth in non-ordinary dimensions. With every breath you take, remember to uplift heart and mind to the sacred. Thank you, Spirit of Air, for your gifts.* (Representative of Air hands (Name) the symbol of air and paints a vertical mark on his chin.

The Element of Metal – *Metal is the symbol of what we make of ourselves. It is the catalyst for change. As you were given this pure form of metal, mold it and shape it, wisely. Thank you, Spirit of Metal, for all your gifts.* (Representative of Metal hands (Name) the symbol of metal and paints a vertical mark down his nose.)

The Representatives of the Five Elements are seated. (Name is asked to stand)

(Name) *You have passed through all the elements of life to return to find your balance. When you feel out of balance, return to the Five Elements and discover which one is too strong or too weak in the present situation. Then using one of your symbols, return yourself to balance.*

> *When you became a man, you put off childish things. As you become a Healer, you must put off separation, fear, short-sightedness, and single-mindedness and embrace oneness, love, long vision, and whole-heartedness. It is time to be that alignment of heart, mind, spirit and body that makes us fully human, so you may teach us how to live in beauty.*

> *Please stand now and place your hands over your heart to make your pledge. Do you accept whole-heartedly your role as Wise Man and the Healer Who Knows? Do you pledge yourself to be of service, to listen with compassion, and speak the wisdom from your heart? Do you dedicate the rest of your life to this healing work, always learning, growing and sharing? Then answer, "I do."*

> *Please cup your hands together in front of your heart and listen with heart, mind and spirit to this charge of your commitment to serve:*

> Within my hands and heart I hold the family of life.
> Within my hands and heart I hold the true spirit of giving.
> Within my hands and heart I hold knowledge of past and future.
> Within my hands and heart I hold the selflessness of sacrifice.
> Within my hands and heart I hold the hopes and prayers of life.
> Within my hands and heart I hold all my relations.
> Within my hands and heart I hold healing.
> May I be worthy of my pledge.

> *O Great Spirit, thank you, for the gift of this Wise Man. Thank you, ancestors, spirit guides, teachers, masters and all helpers who have gathered here with us today. Thank you, Spirits of the Four Directions and Spirits of the Five Elements. We are so grateful for your ever- present love in our lives. Be with us always. We release you now with hearts full of gratitude. And, so it is.*

Will all our Wise Men please rise? We honor you also and give you our gratitude for guiding and leading us in the ways of Truth. We thank the Great Spirit for your life and for your life among us. Will these Wise Men now give a personal blessing to our new Wise Man?

(Full Name), please rise to accept this gift (belt buckle, or other gift) from your spiritual family. May it remind you that each part of creation has a role in the Great Circle of Life. (Wise Men lead (Name) around the Circle and out to close this ceremony)

Other gifts are presented to the new Wise Man and refreshments are served.

MARRIAGE AND COMMITMENT CEREMONIES

To create a personal and unique Marriage Ceremony, please refer to the section on *Creating Your Own Ceremonies* for the Order of Service and notes. Suggestions for creating a Holy Union Ceremony and a Renewal of Marriage Vows Ceremony are also found in that section.

PARTING CEREMONY

There are many reasons that couples part ways. They are often left feeling that something is missing and the part that is missing is sacred closure. This ceremony was created to help couples release the old relationship, so they can each move forward to a new life. In order to experience the fullness of the spiritual releasing, both parties should come to the ceremony with an open heart and a desire to forgive.

If only one of the persons desires to do the ceremony, he or she is committing to the process for themselves and no other negative actions will be taken against the other person. All thoughts and acts of hurt will be transformed to kindness and compassion. All negative comments from friends and family will be diffused and transformed to compassion and understanding.

Supplies: A candle and lighter; 6 small pieces of paper, 2 of, green, blue and pink; two pens; a gift for the other person; a receptacle to hold the burning papers.

Instructions: The couple can perform this ceremony with a mutual friend to lead the ritual or perform it with just the two of them. Choose a quiet, neutral place and light the candle.

Leader: This is the time of parting and releasing. This is the time of choosing new lives. (Names) come together in this place and in this time to ask for forgiveness for any hurt done to the other and to be forgiven. They come to release the old ways of reacting to the other and embrace a new kind and compassionate way. They come to bless the other person as they move forward to their new life. (Names), please face each other and join hands.

Forgiveness

Each person says the words of forgiveness written here or from the heart:

I am sorry that I perceived you as anything less than the wonderful spiritual person that you are. Please forgive me for any unkind thoughts, cruel words or hurtful actions I have done toward you. I am truly sorry that the love we shared together at the beginning changed into something neither of us wanted.

I forgive you and promise that I will only see you as a beloved Child of the Divine from this time forward.

Each person takes a piece of green paper symbolizing forgiveness, lights it from the candle and places it in the receptable to seal the act of forgiveness as the old hurts dissolve in the flame.

Releasing

Each person says the words of releasing written here or from the heart:

I (Name) now release you (Name) from any promises made to me in the past that may keep me from letting you go. I release myself from any promises I made to you in the past. I release you now. I release you to your new life.

Each person takes a piece of blue paper symbolizing releasing and lights it from the candle and places it in the receptacle to seal the act of releasing, as the old life and any old promises dissolve in the flame.

Reframing

Each person says the words of reframing written here or from the heart:

I (Name) now see you (Name) with new eyes, hear your words with new ears, and understand you with a new heart. I bless you as you follow your new path alone that takes you to the unfolding of the Divine Plan for your new life. We are now separate Children of the Divine. We are forever connected through spiritual bonds in the web of life, but no longer entangled in this physical world. Bless you, (Name) on your new path.

Each person takes a piece of pink paper symbolizing reframing and lights it from the candle and places it in the receptable to seal the act of reframing as the old path together burns away with the fire.

Each person then presents the token gift of appreciation to the other person:

I give you this gift as a reminder of all the happy and good times that we have shared as we walked together. Now we walk alone into a happy future.

Leader: *(Names) have forgiven each other and released each other to their new lives. They have exchanged tokens of appreciation and sealed this parting with kindness. May the Great Spirit bless them both now and forever more. And, so it is.*

BLESSING HOME CEREMONY

Many religious traditions and spiritual paths recognize the time of transition from the physical world to the spiritual world as a sacred time. This blessing ritual is to help the person's spirit release the last bonds holding the spirit to the physical body by blessing the body and recognizing the Truth of their spiritual meanings. The ceremony is similar to a Last Rites ritual or Final Prayers.

It is performed for a person close to making the transition and stepping through the door from the physical world to the world of the spiritual. It can also be performed for someone is recently deceased before the body is taken for funeral arrangements. Family and friends can be witness to this blessing home. The Blessing Home is a quiet, sacred, and holy ritual.

Supplies: A candle and a lighter, a small angel to leave with the family, a sacred scarf or stole, anointing oil or olive oil. Soft music may be played in the background.

Instructions: Light the candle and place the angel close by. Lay the sacred scarf or stole on the person's shoulders. (Small willow branches may also be used or a single rose without the thorns)

Opening

Officiant: Dear One, we are gathered here in Love to bless you on your journey home. You are surrounded by the Love of your family and friends on this side and the Love that is radiating from those who have gone before you, calling you from the other side.

Let us pray: *Holy Spirit, be with (Name) as he/she steps through the doorway to return home to You. Be with (Name) and give him/her peace to release the things of this earth and strength to walk in spirit back to the world of Light. Send your Angels to guide his/her feet as this earthly body is shed and the true body of Light embraced once more. Be with all who have gathered here to support (Name) on this journey. Give them comfort and the knowledge that all is well and that soon (Name) will back in the arms of Your great Love. And, so it is.*

Blessing Home

Officiant: *Receive these blessings for your body in the life you leave behind and blessings for your Eternal Spirit and your true body of Light.*

Officiant puts a small amount of oil on his/her fingers and gently touches the part of the body to be blessed. More sensitive parts of the body are not touched. The hand is held 6-8 inches away. As each part is blessed, Officiant seals off the physical energies allowing the spiritual energies to be fully present.

> *Bless these feet that have walked the path of goodness.*
> *Bless this sacral, the foundation of your physical joy.*
> *Bless this solar area that has allowed you to feel the power of God.*

Bless this heart that has always been full of Love and Compassion.
Bless these hands that have served others so well and have worked to make the world a better place.
Bless this throat which has sung the Music of your Soul.
Bless these lips that have spoken the Truth in Love.
Bless these cheeks that have turned away hatred and embraced Love.
Bless these nostrils that have breathed in the Light and breathed out the Love.
Bless these eyes that have seen through the darkness into the real world of Truth.
Bless this forehead that radiated the Truth of your Being.
Bless this crown that held your true Spirit and is now ready to open and release your Spirit back to God.

Bless you, Dear One, for the beautiful life you led, for your caring and for reaching out to help others, for being such a good friend and precious member of this family and for teaching us through the living of your life that we are all Children of the Divine.

May your journey home be peaceful, and may you greet the new day in the arms of your Loving Father-Mother-God surrounded by your loved ones. You are now sealed in Light for your journey home. And, so it is.

Candle is blown out and the angel presented to the family.

MEMORIAL CEREMONY WITH ROSE PETAL RITUAL

A service to celebrate the life of a person who has passed on is a positive way to remember the good and beautiful about a person's life. This ceremony can be performed in a church, hall, funeral home, family home or outdoors. It is an important part of life to celebrate as is birth. Both experiences are sacred. Death comes to all of us just as life comes to all of us. Both experiences are part of the Great Circle of Life. And just as we celebrate birth, so too should we celebrate death, not as an ending, but the great beginning of a new Circle of experience. For death is that doorway that takes us Home again. Everyone's life should be celebrated, no exceptions.

Memorial Services are also a time for spiritual closure to comfort the hearts of those who grieve. A modern addition to the end of life ceremony is a slide show with pictures from the life of the person often set to music. A family friend or the funeral home may put this together. The body of the deceased or the ashes may or may not be present for this ceremony.

Supplies: A candle and lighter, special music, guest book, flowers, photo display, rose petals with two baskets.

Instructions: Begin the ceremony with special music followed by the lighting of the candles. Readers for the Special Readings and the Obituary are selected by the family in advance or may be read by the Leader. Place the rose petals in one basket and place the empty basket beside it.

ORDER OF THE CEREMONY

Welcome

Leader: We come together this day to celebrate the life of our beloved (Name). This is a joyful celebration for this precious Child of the Divine, who was a Light in the World. We celebrate with happy memories and laughter even among the tears for each life given by the Creator is a gift to the world.

Prayer of Assurance

Let us pray. *Heavenly Mother-Father-God, we lift our eyes and our hearts from the shadows of this earth that we might perceive the Light that fills all space and time. We are comforted by Your Indwelling Spirit within us that knows our Beloved (Name) is on his/her way home to the Light. Reach out to him/her and take him/her into your loving arms, surround him/her with your blissful peace. Assured of Your presence we are held fast by the radiance, strength and peace that is life in all realms. (Name) rests now in the serenity of that peace and will soon awaken into the joyfulness of your eternal Love.*

Bring comfort to his/her beloved family (family members may be named) and to all his/her family that cherish him/ her in their hearts. Bring comfort also to his/her friends that have loved him/ her as a sister/brother and a teacher. (Bring comfort to this church family who will miss his/her spirit-filled presence.)

We know that You are the Spirit of Love and Life and we thank You for sharing with us that Holy and Sacred Light through your son/daughter, (Name). And, so it is.

Special Reading

(Special Readings may be shared here, ones that were important to the deceased, to the family, or chosen by the family).

Testimony of Life

A summary of the Highlights of the deceased life is shared here focusing on the spiritual aspects or a testimony from a family member or dear friend.

Special Reading

A Second Reading is shared. (Suggestion: "Speak to me of Death" from the Prophet by Kahlil Gibran)

Special Music

(CD music is also appropriate to be played.)

Obituary

The obituary is read, which appeared in the newspaper or other publication.

Sharing Memories

Members of the family and friends are invited to share a memory of (Name). (Take time to allow everyone who wishes to share the opportunity to speak.)

Prayer of Blessing

Let us pray. *Spirit of the Living God, receive our beloved (Name) into your everlasting arms of Love. Bless him/her with inner peace, serenity and true joy. May good attend every step he/she takes onward into your Kingdom of Light as he/she returns to his/her true Home. Bless those who remain behind and give us the grace to know that one day we shall join him/her in the brilliance of your Light and Love to shine once more together, this time among the stars.*

Ceremony of the Rose Petals

The Ceremony of the Rose Petals comes from the traditions of the Earth based spiritual paths.

Leader: A few sentences from one person cannot describe the depth and breadth of a man's/woman's life, just as these rose petals cannot tell us all about the roses they once blessed. The rose petals represent the qualities and the memories of (Name) that we will remember. I invite you to select a few rose petals from the basket, bless them and then place the petals in the second basket. After the service, the family will take the petals down to the River and with prayerful gratitude for the life of (Name) send them out into the world floating on the loving current of the River to bless the world.

Closing Prayer

Leader: We now commit the body of (Name) back to the earthly elements and his/her spirit to the angelic realm of heaven where he/she will watch over all his/her beloved ones. Receive him/her now, Heavenly Spirit, with great joy in his/her heart as he/she is lifted up from the mountain top on eagle's wings to truly dance once more.

Blessing Home

And now receive this blessing:

May God bless you and keep you and make His face to shine upon you. May the Goddess be gracious unto you and lift up her countenance upon you; and may the Holy Spirit give you peace, now and forevermore. Go now in Peace.

Notes: The Rose Petal Ceremony may be moved to the end of the service as attendees exit.

Community Ceremonies and Blessings

COMMUNITY CEREMONIES AND BLESSINGS

Community rituals and ceremonies are important to the spiritual and physical life of the members. Families can use these ceremonies as well. It is important to recognize the value of the members of our communities and to honor them. Respect comes from this practice of recognizing the value of each human being, no matter their contribution. Everyone has something to contribute to the healthy life of the community.

HONORING OUR ELDERS

Traditional cultures hold their Elders in the very highest esteem. They make sure that every Elder has enough to eat, shelter, and warm clothes and blankets. Elderhood is a special time when we come into full consciousness of our healing powers. We now have the wisdom to put all our knowledge and experience into helping the world. Our Elders represent the best of who we are. Our Elders are living treasures and we are blessed just by being in their presence. They provide us with inspiration, hope, and wise counsel.

Supplies: Candle and lighter; special gifts for all the Elders present.

Instructions: Elders are asked to sit in a place of honor in the room facing the group. (This ceremony can be done in a group, community, or family.)

Opening

Leader: We honor our Elders today as representatives of the Higher Wisdom and Truth of the Creator. We honor our grandmothers and grandfathers as a symbol of honoring all the grandmothers and grandfathers in every family. Let us begin with a prayer.

O Great Spirit Divine, who created the heavens and the earth and all that dwells here, we give thanks for this opportunity to honor our Elders. We ask your blessings upon them. Continue to fill them with your Grace and Love. Thank you for giving them to us to love and to cherish. Thank you for teaching us your great wisdom through them. In honoring our Elders, we honor your Spirit that fills them with such radiance. Thank you, Great Spirit, thank you for our Elders. And, so it is.

Our Dear Elders, we honor you today for your life; for all you have been through; for all you have sacrificed for us. We thank you for all you have done and all you have given to help those whose lives you have touched, your families, your friends, your community. You are our beloved Grandmothers and Grandfathers and we appreciate you so very much. Your light shines brightly in our lives. We bless you and we love you.

Gratitude and Blessings

Let us now show our respect for our Elders by coming forward one at a time, gently taking the hands of each Elder and saying thank you and giving a blessing to each one.

Gifting

Leader: We present you with these gifts as you have gifted us with your presence in our lives. We give you these gifts as a symbol of our love for you. They come from all of us, your children and your grandchildren. As we honor you today, we honor all the Elders around the world. You are all a gift to us from the Creator. (Gifts are presented to the Elders)

Closing

As we close this ceremony, you are invited to be mindful of the Elders who will come into your life this next week. Take the opportunity to say thank you and bless them.

And now our Beloved Elders, may God the Creator, the Spirit of Divine Wisdom and Love, bless you and keep you and hold you in serenity and peace. And, so it is.

The group may sing an appropriate closing song.

BLESSING OF THE CHILDREN

Children receive awards and recognition for their achievements in academics or sports. They rarely receive blessings or recognition for the important role they play in our society as the hope of our future and the manifestation of our dreams. We often forget they are the spiritual links from one generation to the next. This ceremony reminds adults of the importance of our children and that it does take a village to raise a child. All children are our children, our future.

Supplies: An inspirational reading about children, a gift for each child; a space that will hold a large circle; children's songs.

Instructions: After a few words about children and the first song, the group forms a circle. The children take one step to the inside of the circle facing the adults on the outside. The adults repeat their promises to take care of the children. The adults move around the circle taking each child's hand and giving their personal blessing to each. Each child then takes the hand of one adult and brings them into the inside of the circle. (Everyone is clapping during this time). The children keep choosing until all the adults are inside the circle with the children. Then everyone steps back and makes a big circle and sings the "Hokey Pokey." The children are then given their gifts.

Opening

Leader: It is our pleasure to bless the children today. (An inspirational reading about children is shared.)

Just look around at all the beautiful children we have in our spiritual family. Can you see the face of God in them? Now turn to your adult neighbors and see the face of God in them. Let your Inner Child recognize their Inner Child. Holding all these children in our hearts, let's sing our first Inspirational Song. ("He's Got the Whole World in His Hands.")

Children are our messengers to the future. Through their lives, we live on. Through the understandings we teach them, we help make the future world a better place for all humankind. We are each a part of the great chain of humanity, each of us a link that connects the first men and women with all the future men and women through our children. Each link is important, for if one breaks, the chain falls apart. So today we honor and bless and strengthen the links our children represent as they stretch out into the future world and take with them our messages of peace, hope and love.

As we bless the children with us today, we also bless all the children in our families and we bless our own Inner Child. In blessing our children, we acknowledge they are children of God and deserve the richest blessings from God, from the persons responsible for their growth and development, and from each and every one of us. We celebrate each child's life as a special gift from God. It takes a community to raise a child. We love you, our beloved children.

Let us pray. *Father-Mother-God, Creator of all life, thank you for our Inner Child, for the children of our community and for all the children in the world. Keep them safe and strong and fill them with joy and peace that they will always remember who they are. Guide and protect them and open their minds to learning the Truth that we are all Your Children – Children of the Light. And, so it is.*

Circle Gathering

Leader: Let's all form a large Circle together. Will the children now take one step forward into the center of the Circle and turn around to face the adults. Reaching into our hearts now all the adults will say these words with a great outpouring of love for these beloved children before us, for our own Inner Child, for our own children and grandchildren, and for all the children of the world.

Repeat after me:

> We promise to support you
> as your spiritual family
> in every way we can
> to be here to help you
> to work with you
> to play with you
> to love and to cherish you
> to teach and sustain you
> to keep you safe
> and to bless you.
> You are our precious children
> and our hope for the future
> May God bless you and keep you always.

The grownups will now move around the Circle, gently take each child's hand if they are willing, and bless each child in turn.

Each child now chooses someone from the outer Circle to bring into the Inner Circle with them. (Clapping hands during this time.) Keep choosing until all the people in the outer Circle are standing in the Inner Circle.

Leader: *Look around. We are one family, inclusive and caring, and we stand together in this Great Circle of Love. We have a special gift for all the children here today and you will be given your gift at the end of the service. These are to remind you to have fun and be happy and that you are loved by all your spiritual family.*

Everyone steps back to form a large Circle and sings "The Hokey-Pokey."

Gifts are then given to all the children to end the ceremony.

BLESSING OF THE WOMEN

Women are representatives of the Sacred Heart of the Divine. They are the receptive force in the universe. Honoring and blessing women through ceremony helps us recognize the value of the feminine force in our society. Perhaps, with more blessing ceremonies, society will soon realize the great importance of women, not only physically, but spiritually. Women are the living representatives of the Goddess, the Great Mystery of Life, who gives of her own body and soul to give us life, nourishing, supporting and loving us. Women not only create and carry life within them, but they are the creators of Home, that indescribable place of comfort and peace for which we all yearn. The Goddess is the Heart Self of each of us and it is only through our Heart Self that we can truly know the Divine. When we honor our women, we honor our hearts, and we honor the nurturing nature of the Divine. Women are the complement to Men. They are our important connection to the Inner World.

This is an especially moving ceremony when presented on Mother's Day or other women's holidays. The ceremony can be done to bless the women in a family or in a community.

Supplies: Altar cloth, three red candles and a lighter, a bottle of pure water, a special goblet or cup, a crystal pitcher or vase, bouquet of roses of different colors, one to be given to each woman after the ceremony, small paper cups on a tray, one for each member of the gathering.

Instructions: Place the altar cloth on a table with the three red candles and the lighter. Open the bottle of water and place it alongside the goblet and pitcher or vase. Place the vase of roses in the middle.

Opening

Leader: We come together this day to honor and bless all the women of our community and the world as the embodiment of the grace, beauty, and love of the Goddess aspect of the Great Mystery of Life. Women are the creators and carriers of life. They are also the creators of that indescribable place of comfort and peace we call home. Women represent the heart and when we honor women, we honor our own hearts, and the nurturing power of the Divine.

Let us begin with a prayer: *Heavenly Father-Mother God (or the Goddess), be present with us as we honor our women and our hearts today. Bless them with your presence and your guidance that they may come more fully into their sacredness and their gifts. Be with them as they fulfill their purpose to be the directing force for Love. And, so it is.*

In this ceremony we use water, which has long been a symbol of the Goddess. Water symbolizes fluidity, gentle steadfastness that can shape mountains, the ebb and flow of tides, and the very foundation of Life. It is fitting that we use water in this Blessing Ceremony for we are made of water. Into this goblet each woman will pour a little pure water, bless it, and then, pour it into the crystal vase to mingle with the water blessed by all the other women. At the end of this ceremony we will each partake of the water blessed by the women.

The delicate rose is a symbol of perfection and beauty. Our gift to each Woman today is a rose to remember that they are a part of the Great Mystery of Life. The roses are in a vase together during this ceremony to remind us that women are even more beautiful when they bloom together. Each woman will choose a rose at the end of the service to take home with her.

Women are the weavers of life. They use the warp and weft of experiences to weave us all together in Love. The Goddess weaves with three faces, the Maiden, the Mother, and the Wise Woman. We honor the three faces of the Goddess on this special day by first lighting the Goddess candles that represent her three faces. Please stand while the candles are lighted. (The Leader may light the three candles or three women representing the three faces may light the candles.) You may be seated.

Honoring the Women

Leader: We honor first the Maiden Aspect of the Goddess. Will all the women age 17 and younger please come forward? (If no maidens are present, any mother or grandmother may step forward) The Maidens, the young girls, are the hope of our future. They represent the promise of goodness, love and peace that is to come. They are the embodiment of our Nature spirit that connects us to all living things. The young Maidens are symbols of transformation. They are the builders of the chrysalis that will one day transform not only themselves, but all of us into realizing our true form. They are the caretakers and Healers of the Heart. Blessed be the Maidens.

As the Maidens bless the water, let us silently send them our blessings. (Each maiden or representative pours a little pure water into the goblet, blesses it, and then pours it into the vase.) The Maidens may take their seats. *Thank you, Maidens, we are your sisters and brothers. We hold you in the Light of Joy.*

Next, we honor the Mother Aspect of the Goddess. Will all the women over the age of 18 and under the age of 55, please come forward. Mothers are the nurturing and life- giving face of the Goddess. They are the living symbols of the Great Mystery of Birth that brings spirit into form. Our Mothers give of themselves so that we might live. We will never know all they have sacrificed for us. Mothers are our first Teachers and Guides to the inner self. They teach us about the connectedness of all life and our place in the Divine Plan. They teach us about relationships and intimacy. They encourage and nurture us to become the best that we can be. They are the caretakers and Healers of the Mind and the Body. Blessed be the Mothers.

As the Mothers bless the water, let us silently send them our blessings. (Each Mother pours a little water into the goblet, blesses it, and then pours it into the vase.) The Mothers may take their seats. *Thank you, Mothers. We are your children. We hold you in the Light of Love.*

The third face of the Goddess is the Wise Woman, the Grandmother. Will all the women over the age of 55 please come forward. The Grandmothers carry our wisdom, our compassion, and our truth. They are our wise mentors and our spiritual guides. They help us see the larger picture of who we are and point us toward our purpose. They are the Guardians of the Great Mysteries. They are the Gatekeepers of Eternity. They are the Caretakers and Healers of the Soul. Blessed be the Wise Women.

As the Grandmothers, the Wise Women bless the water, let us silently send them our blessings. (Each Grandmother pours a little water into the goblet, blesses it, and then pours it into the vase.) The Grandmothers may take their seats. *Thank you, Wise Women, our Beloved Grandmothers. We are all your grandchildren. We hold you in the Light of Peace.*

Closing

To close our ceremony, will the women please move to the open space and form a circle? The men will take their place in a circle on the outside of the women. The women will first pass the "Joy of the Goddess" to each other by taking the hands of the woman standing next to you and saying, "May the Joy of the Goddess be with you," and the response is "And also with you." The joy is passed to the next woman.

When this is completed, the men will move around the circle gently placing a hand on the woman's shoulder and whispering a personal blessing to each woman. When the blessings are complete, the men join the circle and the tray of cups is brought in with the blessed water from the vase divided between them all. Each person takes a cup, repeats the blessing, and takes a sip of the water drinking it all after the last blessing.

> Blessed be all Maidens. (Circle repeats.)
> Blessed be all Mothers. (Circle repeats.)
> Blessed be all Wise Women. (Circle repeats)
> Blessed be all the Children of the Goddess. (Circle repeats)
> And so it is

Note: We like to throw our empty cups into the middle of the circle when we are finished just for fun.

BLESSING OF THE MEN

Men are representatives of the Divine Masculine, the Sacred Mind. Men are the directive force in the Universe, the great heroes, who follow their passion to the highest level. They are the foundation of the physical as they explore and learn more about the world of form and senses. It is important that we honor men for they carry the wisdom of experience, the spiritual understanding of honor and the integrity of personal moral behavior. They teach us self-discipline, how to harness the great power of emotions for good, to use higher reason, and are models for independence and self-fulfillment. They are the protectors of the world.

When the Sun God came to the world out of the Russian Steppes, he brought strength of body and keenness of mind. He came riding a swift horse and brought a new kind of order. Men are the representatives of that ancient Sun God, who brings energy and power to life. Men are the complement to Women. They are the bridge to the Outer World.

This is a powerful ceremony for celebrating Father's Day or to honor men at other important men's celebrations. The men of a family can be honored or the men in the community.

Supplies: Bottle of sparkling juice; goblet and pitcher or vase; gifts for each man; small paper cups on a tray, one for each member gathered, one large "sun" candle.

Instructions: Place the altar cloth on a table with the sun candle and the lighter. Open the bottle of sparkling juice and place it alongside the goblet and pitcher or vase. Place a basket with the men's gifts in the center.

Opening

We bless our men today as representatives of the Sacred Mind. Men teach us about the outer world and are a bridge to the physical world. They teach us how to live in this world of form, the correct principles for relationship with all its aspects, and how to walk in honor upon the earth. They carry the wisdom of experience, the spiritual understanding of honor and the integrity of personal moral behavior. They are the protectors of the world.

Let's begin our blessing service with a prayer. *Heavenly Father-Mother God, be present with us as we honor our fathers and our men today. Bless them with your presence and your guidance that they may come more fully into their sacredness and their gifts. Be with them as they fulfill their purpose to be the directing force for peace. And, so it is.*

Wine represents the masculine, for it is a transformed symbol of the outer world. Wine is more than the grapes it comes from. In the process of adding spices and letting the grapes ferment over time, they are changed to become more than what they were at the beginning of their lives. It is fitting that we use wine (this sparkling juice) in this ceremony for through our understanding of what it means to be a man, we are all transformed. Into this goblet each man will bless his share of the sparkling juice and pour it into the pitcher to blend with the blessings of all the other men here today.

Our Gifts this year to our men are (gifts of choice). We honor our men today with these gifts. They will be presented at the end of the ceremony.

Men are represented by the Sun, the powerful force of the burning stars. Our sun candle represents this Divine force and we light it in honor of all men everywhere who are the heroes, the active leaders, the rock on which the family is built. Please stand as the sun candle is lighted. You may be seated.

The Divine Masculine has three faces: Explorer, Sacred Warrior and Shaman. Each man passes through each of these stages as he grows. In many religions and spiritual paths, God is portrayed as masculine. It is the masculine qualities of God that we also honor today through God's expression in men.

First, we honor the Explorer face of the God. Will all the young men under the age of 18 please come forward? If we have no Explorers with us today, any man can step forward to represent the Explorers of his family. If there are no men to represent the Explorers, any woman may step forward. The young Explorers represent that part of God that reaches out into this world to learn everything about it. The Explorers represent the vanguard of God, those who take the first step into the unknown. The Explorers find the water when we are thirsty, bring us food when we are hungry, and lead us to safety when we are afraid. They will climb the mountains to see what is at the very top, shoot out into space to see the stars, explore every aspect of life to see where we fit into the Great Circle. And they open their tender hearts to bear incredible sorrow for us. They are the Caretakers and Healers of the Heart.

As the Explorers bless the juice, let us silently send them our blessings. Each Explorer pours a little juice into the goblet, blesses it, and then pours it into the vase. The Explorers may take their seats. *Thank you, Explorers. We are all your brothers and sisters. We hold you in the light of Truth.*

Next, we honor the Sacred Warriors. Will all the men 18 years old and under the age of 55 please come forward? If we have no Sacred Warriors with us today, any man may come forward to represent them. If we have no men present, any woman may step forward as representative. The Sacred Warriors represent the Father face of the God, whether they have had children or not. The Fathers are the Sacred Warriors, protecting and guiding us along the physical paths to see the Great Spirit everywhere. They are the strong hands that pick us up when we fall, comforting us until we are ready to go on again. They are the leaders, the great thinkers, the rock and supporters of the family. They are the keepers of the stories of our families. They teach us about our inner and outer resources, how to work together for the greater good, and to use our dreams to reach our goals. They are the Caretakers and Healers of the Mind and Body.

As our Fathers, our Sacred Warriors bless the juice, let us silently send them our blessings. Each Sacred Warrior pours a little juice into the goblet, blesses it, and then pours it into the vase. The Sacred Warriors may take their seats. *Thank you, Sacred Warriors. We are all your children. We hold you in the Light of Honor.*

The Grandfathers, the Shamans are the third face of God. Will all the men over age 55 please come forward? If there are no men over 55, any man may step forward as representative. If there are no men, any woman may step forward. The Grandfather, the Wise Man, the Shaman, carries the experience of years to share with us. They are our Teachers, our Mentors, our Wisdom. They help us see how to help ourselves, reminding us that we are Divine and a part of the Great Medicine Wheel of Life. They are the Messengers of the Mystery. They are the bridge between the physical world and the world of spirit. They teach us through the loving example of their own lives. They are the Caretakers and Healers of the Soul.

As our Wise Men, our Grandfathers bless the juice, let us silently send them our blessings. Each Grandfather pours a little juice into the goblet, blesses it, and then pours it into the vase. The Wise Men may take their seats. *Thank you, Grandfathers and Shamans. We are all your grandchildren and students. We hold you in the Light of Wisdom.*

Now the women will form two lines facing inward. The men will walk through the lines one at a time. The women will gently touch each man on the back or shoulder and whisper their blessings as we honor the Men of our Community as representatives of all Men everywhere. (Men go through the blessing line walking slowly to receive their blessings.)

Let us now form a circle and pass the cups of juice. We will repeat each blessing followed by a sip of juice, drinking the remaining juice after the fourth blessing.

> Blessed be all Explorers. (Circle repeats) (Take the first sip)
> Blessed be all Sacred Warriors. (Take the second sip)
> Blessed be all Shamans. (Take the third sip)
> Blessed be all the children of the God. (Drink the remaining juice)
> And, so it is.

BLESSING OF THE ANIMALS

Animals are our brothers and sisters, our companions who are a part of the God's creation. They are animal companions entrusted to us to care for and to love. Not only are we to care for these companions but for all of God's creation, the two-legged, the four-legged, the many-legged, the beings that swim and the beings that fly. We are all family on this our Mother the Earth and we humans are the older brothers and sisters. We are all part of the Great Circle of Life.

Supplies: Water in a bowl, treats for dogs and cats, donation basket, certificates of blessing, (optional).

Instructions: It is best to have this ceremony in a park or large yard, so the animals can move around. It is also better to have the animals on a leash or in a cage. They can be taken out for the blessing time, if it is safe to do so. Children can bring stuffed animals to be blessed or photographs of deceased animals. Animals, too difficult to bring, can also be blessed through photographs.

Introduction

Leader: We are gathered today to bless our animas and pet companions. St. Francis of Assisi, whose birthday we celebrate on Oct 5th, taught us to love the other beings that live with us on this earth. He talked to the animals and the birds and they in turn shared with him a greater understanding of the unity of all life. It is in his honor that people all over the world bless the animals at this time of year.

In honor of our beloved companions, we are making donations to the (Local animal protection society or another animal agency). The donation basket will be here for you to make your donation after the blessings. Every donation helps the animals in our community which are in need. Next to the donation basket are some treats. Please take one for your friend after the blessing.

Ceremony

There is a special bond between people and animals that can never be broken. These animals are not pets; they are beloved companions sharing our lives, our hopes and our dreams, showing us unconditional love. They make us laugh and they make us cry. They often give our lives purpose. We have much to learn from these companions and it is fitting that we should bless them.

Let us pray: *Holy Creator, you alone can make all things new. Send your Holy Spirit upon us and give us new hearts to feel, new ears to hear, and new eyes to see the unity of all beings in your grand Creation. Bless our animal companions with good health and happiness, with joy and love. Bless all our pets that have gone on before us. We know they will be waiting to greet us when we cross over. Bless this water as a symbol of your Love and our love for these wondrous beings as we use it to bless them. And, so it is.*

Before we begin the blessing of the animals, I ask that each one of you renews your promise to your animal friend. Please look at your pet as you make these promises.

Do you promise to give your friend only kindness, friendship, affection and caring? **I do.**

Do you promise to treat your friend as one of God's creations and hold it dear to your heart? **I do**.

Do you promise to love and care for your animal friend to the best of your ability and to never mistreat your friend only to guide and cherish? **I do**.

Pat your animal friend with great affection.

Leader blesses each of the animals by dipping the fingers into the bowl of water and gently touching the top of the pet's head. Bless the children's stuffed animals and the photographs. (Give Owners the Blessing Certificates, optional).

Go now in peace and love and gratitude for each other. And, so it is.

Remember to pick up a treat for your friend before you leave. Thank you so much for coming and supporting our local animal friends.

COMMUNITY HEALING CEREMONY

Tragedy often occurs in a community and one of the best ways to find comfort is through a healing ceremony for the entire community. These ceremonies are often held at night with lighted candles bringing their healing energy to the hearts of everyone. Music, readings, and memories are important elements for healing ceremonies.

It is best to plan these ceremonies at a time most members of the community can attend. Advanced notice of the ceremony is important, so people will be able to come. They can be held indoors or outdoors. Make sure there is plenty of seating or plan a short ceremony if people will be standing.

Supplies: Candles with protective papers and volunteers to pass them out; special music or musicians; special readings and people who volunteer to do the readings; sound equipment if needed, (set up in advance); chairs.

Instructions: Prepare an Order of Service - the order in which people will sing or read. Invite appropriate dignitaries to be part of the ceremony. The candles are lighted at the end of the service and a final song is sung followed by a blessing.

Order of Service

Soft music is playing while people are coming in.

Welcome and Purpose for Gathering

Leader: We are gathered here this evening as friends and neighbors, to bring comfort and hope to our community. This event has brought not only sorrow to the family, but sorrow to our entire community. We want the family to know that this community supports them and will continue to care. (Add words of comfort as needed.) In these times, we do not understand why this has happened, but we do know that the more we come together as a compassionate community, the stronger we are.

First Reading

First Speaker

Special Music

Second Reading or Prayer

Second Speaker

Special Music - Soloist

Sharing Time

If anyone would like to share a thought or word of comfort, please come forward now.

Candle Lighting

As we light the candles of hope and peace, let us each say our own prayer for _____. Let us join in singing ("Amazing Grace" or other inspiring song).

Candles are lit and group joins in closing song.

Blessing Home

May the peace of God be with_____and with all of us as we move forward helping and serving each other.

ANGEL BLESSING CEREMONY

Angels appear in all religions. They are considered messengers of God. They are Light Beings, but sometimes look like humans. The majority of people worldwide believe in angels and their mission to help us. Angels speak to us on a deeper level – on the level of the heart. Angels help us to remember the Oneness of all life. The more we are aware of the spiritual aspects of being, the more the consciousness of humanity will be in tune with the gifts of the Spirit. Those gifts are represented by the Angels - Love and Compassion, Joy and Peace. And when we reach that level of wholeness of mind, heart, body and spirit, instead of Angels coming to us, we will be able to go to the Angels.

This is a short ceremony that can be added to other ceremonies or services. In this ritual the participants become the voices for the Angels.

Supplies: None. Printed angel blessings to hand out are optional. Quiet angelic music.

Instructions: Form two lines facing each other. Each person will walk slowly between the lines in an attitude of listening to the guidance of the angels who will be speaking through each participant. The people standing in line will reach out in turn and gently touch the person on the arm, whispering the message from the angels just for him or her. When the person reaches the end of the line, he or she will step back into line and be prepared to speak inspired words from the angels to the next person. Continue until every person has walked down the line and been inspired by the angel voices. (Play soft inspirational music during the blessings.)

Leader: We come together to be blessed by the angels. We are each a representative of the angels as we allow them to speak through our voices and share their love through our caring. Let us take a moment in the silence to open our hearts to the angels.

Let us form two lines now facing each other. Close your eyes and take a deep breath and go to your Center of Peace so the angels can speak through your voice. Be open to the inspiration that is coming from your heart as an angelic message is given to each individual. When your turn comes, be receptive to the angel messages just for you.

(Participants walk slowly between the lines allowing time to receive the angel blessings.)

Closing

Leader: *Heavenly Angels, be with us as we become your voices speaking the messages of the Divine for each other.*

(A closing song may be sung.)

DEDICATION AND BLESSING CEREMONY FOR ESTABLISHING A COMMUNITY

A community is a living, breathing sacred gathering of people with a common purpose. Each person is a unique strand of sacred individuality that forms the rich tapestry of the community. Each thread of experience woven together binds those individualities into a wholeness of color, song, thought, feeling, action and relationship. Each time the community comes together it weaves another thread of life.

This is a ceremony to affirm the decisions of the people to be more than just a group. It is an affirmation of the purposes and dedication to come together to work together, to make a difference in the world, and to celebrate diversity through unity. A ceremony binds the community members on a spiritual and heart level.

Prayers to the Seven Directions are used to include all of life outside the community to symbolize that the community does not stand alone.

Supplies: A symbol of the community that can be blessed and given to each member of the community; (Purpose and Mission Statement of Community); a Certificate of Dedication to be signed by all the members; pens and writing surface.

Instructions: The participants gather in a circle, hear the purpose and mission statement of the community, ask blessings from the Seven Directions, pledge their support, and sign the Certificate of Dedication.

Opening

Leader: We are gathered here in this Great Circle to affirm the purpose of our community and dedicate our desire to work together to bring those purposes to the world. As we grow in Spirit and in Truth together, so will our efforts to bring our highest purpose into our own lives and the lives of others. We also dedicate our community to practicing compassion and peace as we continue to honor and respect each other and all life.

Purpose and Mission Statement are read.

Let us pray*: Divine Spirit that is known by Many Names and is working through us as sparks of Creation, we ask your blessings on this community, whose purpose is to bring together the fragments of the One Heart, to learn how to bless each other, and to live in peace and harmony with everyone and everything on this beautiful world. We ask the blessings of the Angels, the Wise Guides, our members in Spirit, all who help us every day to listen to the higher consciousness that dwells within us. Help us to make a new choice for peace and compassion. We pray to become models for peace in our own lives so that our community may be a model for peace for our greater community. We pray that our community is now blessed with the highest good, with strength, love, prosperity, and joy and that each person who comes into our community circle feels this and is blessed. Thank you for these blessings as we pray this day in the Name that we hold Most Holy. And, so it is.*

Seven Directions Blessings

Leader: Please stand and join me in asking for blessings from the Seven Directions for Our Community. Our Community is a Great Circle and we invite the Spirits of all those attuned to our purpose to join us in spirit for this Dedication. The people will respond with *"We pledge ourselves and our Community"* after the prayer for each Direction.

Turn to the East. *We bless the East, the place of new Beginnings, the sunrise of hope and the promise of all things good. The East reawakens us to the Truth of Who We Are. O, East, bless the beginnings of our Community with Light and Love. Bless the beginning of each new thought, word and deed as every journey begins with just one step taken in faith and hope. Aho.*

People: We pledge ourselves and our Community.

Turn to the South. *We bless the South, the place of abundance and prosperity as the seeds we plant grow into Being. The South reminds us to always be thankful for what we are and what we have. O, South, bless the abundance and growth of our Community with Peace and Joy. Bless the abundance of ideas, gifts, and knowledge as we share with one another.* Aho.

People: We pledge ourselves and our Community.

Turn to the West. *We bless the West, the place of harvest of the fruits of our labors. The West is the setting of rich ideas as the sun sets behind the curve of the earth to be reborn again. The West reminds us to cherish that which has passed and to welcome that which is to come. O, West, Bless the harvest of Love and Caring of our Community, and bless each person, who is touched by our Community Spirit.* Aho.

People: We pledge ourselves and our Community.

Turn to the North. *We bless the North, the place of silence and fulfillment. North is the place of waiting and going within to the sacred. The North reminds us that feelings are important, and we should honor all feelings. O, North, Bless the feelings of our Community that our hearts grow in spiritual understanding and be uplifted. May our Community always revere the sacredness of all life. Bless our hearts with wisdom and the fulfillment of Spirit and the peace of Silence.* Aho.

People: We pledge ourselves and our Community.

Turn to the Sky. *We bless the Above, the heavens, the home of the Father, who holds us in His Loving Arms. Our Father reminds us to be strong, to go within to find our answers, and to treat everyone with dignity. Bless our Community, Father, that we can come to you with upturned faces without shame.* Aho.

People: We pledge ourselves and our Community.

Turn to the Earth. *Our Mother the Earth holds us in her Loving Arms, and feeds us from her Heart. Our Mother reminds us to share what we have, to treat other beings with compassion, and to take care of ourselves and our resources. Bless our Community, Mother of us all, that we always remember to love one another, to sustain you and to share your bounty.* Aho.

People: We pledge ourselves and our Community.

Turn to the Center. *Here in the Center of our Community is the sacred Heart of the Divine Spirit. It is a living center, radiating the holy breath into our Community. Wherever we go, whatever we do, this Center is always shining in the Light of the Sacred and we can feel it as a part of us. Bless our Community O Sacred Heart Center, that we realize and touch the sacredness of our lives.* Aho.

People: We pledge ourselves and our Community

Leader: Join hands and repeat after me:

We hereby dedicate this community to the higher and sacred purposes of Peace, Joy, Love, Inclusiveness, and Truth. We dedicate this community to (add in purpose). We pledge to live our values and to support each other and the greater community of life. And, so it is.

Please come forward now and sign your name to this Certificate of Dedication in honor of the pledges we have made to mark this sacred act of dedication.

Note: A simple certificate can be made in advance that states the name of the community, its purpose and mission, and the date it was dedicated. Leave space at the bottom for all the signatures.

Ceremonies and Blessings for Mother Earth

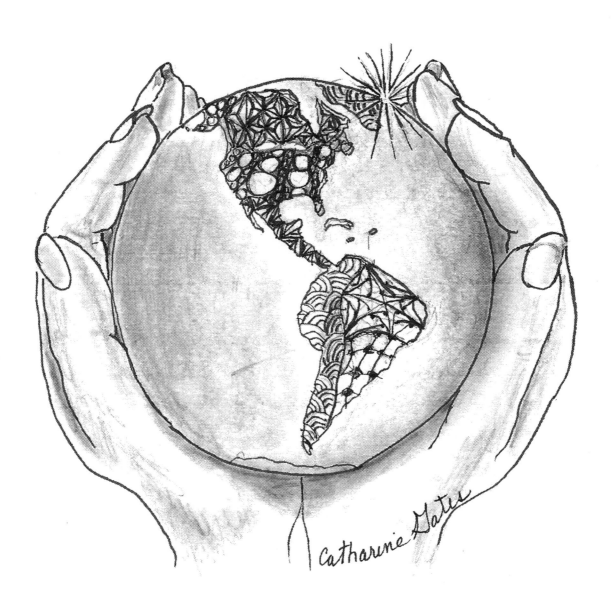

Catharine Gates

CEREMONIES FOR MOTHER EARTH

We are children of Mother Earth, here to experience the beauty and power of this blue planet. We are connected to every other part of the Web of Life and we are a part of the Divine Plan for this world. It is our responsibility to care for the planet which sustains us and provides all our nourishment. We also have a spiritual responsibility to honor Mother Earth through ceremony and ritual. Our daily prayers are filled with thanksgiving for the blessings that Mother Earth bestows upon us.

EARTH DAY CEREMONY

Even though Earth Day is a modern celebration, as Children of Mother Earth we should take time to reflect on how we are taking care of our beloved Mother and to be grateful for all the blessings bestowed upon us for our physical and spiritual health. Earth Day is set for April 22, the Spring Equinox, a time honored by our distant ancestors as the first day of the turning of the season toward new growth and the greening of the world. Earth Day was founded by Senator Gaylord Nelson in 1970 as a grassroots effort to raise awareness about concerns for our environment. It is now celebrated all around the world.

This is a simple ritual that individuals, families, or communities can do to celebrate Mother Earth and make a new commitment to heal and sustain the earth.

Supplies: Eggshells filled with bird seeds (plastic eggs that can be used every year are good bird seed containers); pinecones stuffed with peanut butter; packets of garden seeds.

Instructions: Gather in a circle in a park or a yard or in the heart of the community.

Leader: This is Earth Day, a time to celebrate and bless our Mother the Earth. We are so grateful for the privilege of living here on this beautiful blue planet.

We are the children of Mother Earth. As we stand here in this Circle of Peace we remember the richness of your blessings. Let us take a few minutes to go around the circle and share a blessing of Mother Earth that is important to us.

Mother Earth, we pledge to honor our homes and land that we hold in sacred trust for you. We pledge to preserve the life of this beautiful world. We pledge to care for the green plant people and the trees.

We pledge to care for the tiny insects that live close to and in the soil. We will not kill any living being but find a new home for them to live. We pledge to honor the rocks and minerals and listen to their lessons. We pledge to respect the four-legged and the winged-ones who share the land with us and teach us. We pledge to honor the finned-ones and all the life of the rivers and oceans. We are the two-legged human beings and we are responsible for our brothers and sisters. We pledge to honor and respect each other and to work together to care for you, our Great Mother, sustainer of our lives. We place our hands on our hearts and pledge now to do all these things and more in beauty, harmony, and peace. May we walk in beauty upon this earth. Thank you, Great Mother, for our life. And, so it is.

Eggs are a symbol of new life and an ancient symbol of Mother Earth. Take your egg in your hands and hold it close to your heart, close your eyes and visualize this blue planet Earth as seen from outer space against the dark and star-filled sky.

O Great Creator of the Universe, Creator of all the Stars and Planets and our own Mother Earth, we ask your blessings on our beautiful home. Bless all the beings who live here together. Guide us to treat all our brothers and sisters with kindness and compassion so we may all flourish and grow to become the best we can be. Help us to remember that we are all part of Your Magnificent creation. And, so it is.

The eggs are filled with bird seeds, a symbol of the abundance of life that Mother Earth provides to nourish us all. The pinecones are filled with peanut butter, a substance that binds us all together as one family. Choose an egg and a pinecone, hold them in your hands for a moment as you bless them and then go out into the park and scatter the seeds and place the pinecone in a tree. The birds, the messengers of the Creator, will come and take the blessings out into the world.

When we are finished, we will pick up any litter in this area as a simple way to take care of Mother Earth on this Earth Day. You may do the same when you return home.

Go in peace and walk gently on our Mother.

BLESSING OF THE WATER

Water is a gift from the Creator. Water is precious. Even on a planet covered with water, only one percent is fresh water and available for us to use. We are made of mostly water. Water ebbs and flows in our bodies just like the ocean waves ebb and flow. Our beginnings are in water and our lives flow like water. It is important for us to be mindful of our water and to bless its healing energy.

Water is also a sacred substance that can be infused with spiritual energy and blessings. Water is also a messenger. It carries the energy of our thoughts and feelings. The work of Dr. Masaru Emoto proves that water is a messenger of our thoughts and feelings, prayers and goodwill. He photographs frozen water drops just as they begin to thaw making snowflake crystals in intricate patterns. Water that has received positive thoughts and prayers reveal beautiful, complex, and colorful patterns. Negative thoughts directed towards the water reveal incomplete and ugly patterns.

Bless all the water that you drink. You want to send good, positive and healing messages to your body. You can also set your water glass on a piece of paper with the word LOVE written on it or tape it to the outside of your water bottle.

Supplies: Small containers of water brought from homes; small containers of water collected from nearby lakes, streams and rivers, or the ocean; large pitcher. Containers and empty pitcher are placed on a table together. (Optional – a large piece of paper with the word LOVE written on it to place under the containers of water.)

Instructions: This ceremony can be performed indoors or outdoors by an individual, family or community. The participants may stand in a circle or be seated. Four people or teams are appointed to represent the waters of the four directions who will bring a cup of water from each direction in the ceremony. Children can be on the teams. The Water Carriers take their places in the proper direction as the ceremony begins, with their cups of water ready. One person from each group may be designated to present the reading for the direction or the Leader may do the reading.

Opening

All: Water of Life, bless us, heal us. Thank you, Water of Life. We love you. We care for you.

Leader: Let us pray: *O, Great Creator of Water and of All Life, we ask your blessings on this water that comes from our homes. We ask your blessings on this water that comes from the natural world around us. We ask your blessings on the water that is present in our bodies. We ask your blessings on the water that comes from the four directions of the earth to mingle together this morning as a symbol of the precious gifts we receive from your bounty. Thank you for the precious gift of water. Thank you for the precious gift of life. And, so it is.*

Ceremony of the Four Directions

(Water Carriers of the East come forward.) *Waters of the East, flow into this place, our home, as a promise of new beginnings, as a symbol of the Divine that rises each morning in the East to flood the waters of the world with Light.* (Water is poured into the pitcher and the Water Carriers of the East take their seats).

Leader: *Behold, water now flows from the east into our common home: waters from the ancient cities of the East, waters from the natural springs, waters from the battle grounds, waters from the peaceful fields, waters from the majestic Alps, waters from the great rivers and oceans. Waters of the Earth, waters of life and healing, flow to us from the East.*

All: Bless us, waters, and bring us home.

(Water Carriers of the South come forward.) *Waters of the South, flow into this place, our home, as a promise of the right of all creatures to have clean water, as an emblem of justice and as an act of peace, as* *a symbol of the Divine power abundance and growth.* (Water is poured into the pitcher and the Water Carriers of the South take their seats.)

Leader: *Behold, water now flows from the south into our common home: waters from the emerald islands of the tropics, waters from the frozen lands, waters from the rich land of our birth, from the Nile River; waters from the great pyramids; waters from the lands of mystery, from the tall mountain homes, from the mighty Amazon River. Waters of the Earth, waters of life and healing, flow to us from the South.*

All: Bless us, waters, and bring us home.

(Water Carriers of the West come forward.) *Waters of the West, flow into this place, our home, as a symbol of the setting sun, the land of endings and completion and a full understanding and promise of a new day to be reborn.* (Water is poured into the pitcher and the Water Carriers of the West take their seats.)

Leader: *Behold, water now flows from the West into our common home: waters from the sacred temples of the Orient; waters from the Polynesian islands; waters from the vineyards, waters from the rugged coasts, waters from the fertile forests, from the mighty Colorado and Snake Rivers. Waters of the Earth, waters of life and healing, flow to us from the West.*

All: Bless us, waters, and bring us home.

(Water Carriers of the North come forward.) *Waters of the North, flow into this place, our home, as a symbol of the place where the Light burns within, where we can see our life frozen in time in this sacred place of serenity and peace, where we can sit by the quiet pools and contemplate peace.* (Water is poured into the pitcher and the Water Carriers of the North take their seats.)

Leader: Behold, water now flows from the North into our common home: icy cold waters from the glaciers; from the bay with the highest tides in the world; waters from the woodlands and lakes, water from the Boundary Waters, from Mongolia and Siberia; waters from Greenland's frozen shores; waters from the deep Arctic where life ends and once more begins. Waters of the Earth, waters of life and healing, flow to us from the North.

All: Bless us, waters, and bring us home.

All: *We are One with the Waters of Life. We too are flowing together in this season of new life, and for this we lift our hearts in blessing and thanksgiving. Praise for this water, symbol of our beginning and ending, sign of our power to bless and heal. May our lives pour out this year for the common good, and may our lives together flow as the clearest stream links earth and water and sky. May harmony prevail for our waters. May peace prevail for our waters. May there be peace and harmony for all beings who share the precious water on our beautiful earth. And, so it is.*

Leader: Please come forward now one at a time taking the container of water you brought from your home and/or a natural source close to you, bless your water and pour half of it into the pitcher. When all the water has been blessed and mingled, the Water Pourers of the Four Directions will take the pitcher outside and pour the blessed water into a stream where it will go out into the world carrying the messages of our blessings. (If there is no stream available, pour the water under a tree on a slope) Take the other half of the water you brought today home with you and pour it over your threshold to bless your home and family.

May we ever walk in awe of the wondrous gift of water and hold it in our sacred heart, honoring this gift of Life. Go in peace and flow like the precious waters of the Earth. And, so it is.

BLESSING OF THE TREES

Without the Plant World, we would not be here. The plants were here before we were. The plants and trees are an important part of this world and as humans have expanded, we have taken more and more of their space. They provide more than food for us. They also provide the oxygen we breathe. We have a symbiotic relationship with plants and trees as we exhale the carbon dioxide they need, and they exhale the oxygen we need. We cannot destroy the plants and trees, or we will perish.

This ceremony acknowledges the importance of the plants and trees and shows our honor and respect for this wonderful part of God's creation.

Supplies: Cornmeal in a small container on a small table

Instructions: Gather in a circle in a park, yard, or forest where there are several trees.

Begin the ceremony with drumming or an opening song ("Where I Stand Is Holy")

Chanting the Directions

Leader: We are gathered to bless the trees in our community by blessing these trees. Without the trees we would have no oxygen to breathe or food to eat. They provide wood for our homes and fuel to keep us warm. But more than that they represent the Great Tree of Life with roots that go down into Mother Earth and branches that reach to the heavens. They represent our spiritual connection between earth and sky.

This ritual is based on a Peruvian ritual. We begin by facing the Four Directions (first facing South) and chanting 3 times the name of the deity associated with that direction. This chanting calls in the energy of the direction, the aspect of God that dwells there.

Face the South – Pa-cha-**ma**-ma (Mother Earth)

Face the West – Ma-ma-**kee**-la (Grandmother Moon)

Face the North – Wee-ra-**co**-cha (Father Sun)

Face the East – Mu-yu-**ma**-ru (Grandfather of the Unseen World)

Face the Center – Ku-u-**ee**-chi (The Eternal Rainbow)

Opening Prayer

Let us pray: *O Creator, we come here to this sacred place to offer our blessings to our sisters and brothers of the Plant Kingdom through the trees as a symbol of all green life on our Mother Earth. We know we and others of our kind have destroyed the trees and we now ask forgiveness for these actions. We have not listened to the wisdom of the green beings. We offer this cornmeal and our individual prayers to bless the trees and humbly ask them to carry this message throughout the plant world expressing our gratitude for each and every blade of grass, for each leaf, thorn, stem, flower and fruit. We are grateful for all the sacrifices the trees and plants make so that we may live and grow. We are truly thankful for these gifts. And, so it is!*

Blessing Ceremony

Leader: Stand with your eyes closed, hands relaxed at your sides, and take 4 deep breaths, in through the nose and out through the mouth. Imagine yourself having roots that extend from the base of your spine, down through your legs, out your feet and down into the earth. These roots anchor you and enable you to draw on the Earth's energy as the plants do. Now shift your awareness to a point about 6 inches above your head and imagine a bright light of Radiant energy coming into being. Open your crown chakra to this energy and see it filling you up and flowing over you like a waterfall. Let the Earth's energy and the Radiant light energy become centered in your heart and balanced within you.

When you feel balanced and centered take some cornmeal, move out of this Circle, and begin walking among the trees. When you feel a bond with a specific tree, go toward it and stand in front of it. Lay your hand on its trunk and bless it. Sprinkle a little cornmeal at its base when you are finished and move to the next tree. Keep blessing the trees until you feel a completion and return to the Circle.

Closing Prayer

Leader: *Thank you, Creator of all Life, for giving us the plants and trees that we may live together in harmony and balance. We honor each green being that exists with us here on Mother Earth. We pray for their highest good and are so grateful for the gifts and wisdom they bring us. We affirm to take better care of all the green beings within our Circle of Life. Blessings, Blessings, Blessings to our sisters and brothers of the Plant Kingdom.*

Note: Do this ceremony at home for your own plants and trees or for the plants and trees on your street if you live in the city.

BLESSING OF THE FIELDS

Many cultures bless the fields each year asking for good weather, plenty of rain, and fruitful crops. A suggested date for this ceremony is the second Sunday in March, but it can also be performed before the planting season depending on your area's planting times. The farm equipment and the farmers who till the fields are also blessed. This is an important ceremony for it brings our awareness back to the foundational source of our food, not the grocery stores, but the fields and orchards. This ceremony also helps children understand how the land supports the people. This ceremony can be modified for city dwellers who have gardens or belong to a community garden co-op. (See also the Blessing of the Gardens).

Supplies: Organic marigold flower seeds, (4 will be planted at the side of each field); pure water that has been blessed, a cupful will be symbolically poured onto the soil.

Instructions: This ceremony can be performed for one field symbolizing all the fields in the area or it can be performed for several fields. Arrange in advance which fields will be blessed and ask permission for a few organic marigold seeds to be planted at the side of the field. Gather the people to the side of the field and process just inside the field or to the center of the field, if practical. A song may be sung for the processional or drums may keep the beat. Be mindful of the farmer's land, the phase of the planting (i.e., if the ground has already been tilled and furrowed), and the footwear of the participants.

Leader: We are gathered here as people of the land to bless this field and all the fields of the world that bring forth the crops that feed not only the people, but the other children of the Great Spirit. We ask that you join in this blessing in gratitude for the miracle of life that is at the heart of the seeds that will be planted and harvested in this field.

Blessings from the Four Directions

Please face East: *Spirit of the East, place of the rising sun, we ask your blessings on this field and on all those hands that will help this crop to grow, may the sun shine lovingly on the seeds planted here and may the plants rise in joyful dances to greet each new day. Thank you for the sun rays shining with life.*

Turn South: *Spirit of the South, place of nourishment, we ask your blessings on this filed and on all the hands that will help this crop to grow, may the richness of your soil feed and nurture each seed to bring them to the perfect plant. Thank you for the nourishment, food for the food.*

Turn West: *Spirit of the West, the place where water rises from the great oceans and rides the clouds to bring its live-giving refreshment to the seeds and plants. With your help the seeds will burst into life that will sustain others. Thank you for the waters of life.*

Turn North: *Spirit of the North, the place where time is quiet, where seeds contemplate new life and when they are finished resting, spring into new growth, first sending out roots deep into Mother Earth and then sending up arms to reach for the sky. Thank you for this precious time of resting and transformation.*

Turn Center: *Spirit of All Creation, we give thanks for the Spirits of the Four Directions which manifest your sacred life-giving elements. We pray for good weather, temperate and gentle rains, and nourishment for these seeds. We thank you for the blessings upon this field and all the fields of the world, upon the waters, the sun, and the nutrients in the soil. We thank you for the blessings you bestow upon the people who work* *the land to bring forth the food to feed your people. We thank you for the blessings you give to us and for the beauty of this green world. And, so it is.*

Taking up the seeds: *We bless these flower seeds as the messengers of the sacred life they contain to inspire all the seeds to be planted here to reach their full and sacred potential.* (Plant seeds)

Taking up the cup or water: *We bless this water as the messenger of growth and beauty for this field. May it instill in the waters and rain to come the blessing of the Creator for an abundant crop.* (Pour out water onto the field).

Let us take a few minutes to add our personal blessings for this field and the sacred life to come forth. And, so it is. Our prayers have taken flight, may the rain of blessings fall.

The gathering carefully and reverently walks out of the field to the beat of the drum or an appropriate song.

Note: This ceremony can be modified to a Blessing of the Land with the gathering actually going to the four corners of the land for each blessing of the Four Directions, then back to the middle of the property for the remaining ceremony.

BLESSING OF THE GARDEN

Honoring the Three Sisters

Just as the fields are to be blessed, so the gardens that feed our bodies and provide beauty to feed our spirits, should be blessed. This blessing ceremony should be done after the beds are prepared and before the first seed is planted. Children enjoy taking part in this ceremony. They can even have their own gardens to take care of and enjoy.

Originating with the Haudenosaunee (People of the Long House) this ancient tradition spread from the Six Nations of the Iroquois Confederacy in the northeast across America. This ceremony is based on the tradition of planting the Three Sisters, corn, pole beans, and squash together. Scientists discovered that this ancient planting contributes to the health of all three plants in a unique way. The corn stalks provide support for the climbing beans, which produce nitrogen for the corn. The corn and beans provide shade for the squash, which helps keep the moisture in the soil with its large leaves thus helping the beans and corn. Companion planting is a good teaching tool for children to explain the benefits of "community."

Supplies: Corn, pole beans, and yellow squash seeds; trowel; water; children, (optional.)

Instructions: Prepare the garden beds to receive the seeds. Gather the supplies and the family, say the blessings, and plant the Three Sisters together. Let the children pour the water on the planted seeds.

Opening

Leader: Today we come together to honor our garden and all the gardens all over the world. The soil was gifted to us by the Great Spirit of Life, as were the seeds, the sun and the water, so that we, the people, and all the other creatures could have food. We also honor the Three Sisters who teach us to that we can live together and help each other. We are thankful for our food and this opportunity to watch the miracle of life that the Divine has created.

First, we dig a hole and plant three corn seeds: *Thank you, Sister Corn, for growing into such delicious food for us to eat. We honor you by planting and watering your seeds.* Cover up the seeds and pour water on the hole.

Dig a second hole close to, but not on top of, the corn seeds just planted, and put three bean seeds in the hole: *Thank you, Sister Bean, for growing into such delicious crisp green food for us to eat. We honor you by planting you next to Sister Corn and watering your seeds.* Cover up the seeds and pour water on the hole.

Dig a third hole close to, but not on top of, the other seeds just planted. Put three squash seeds in the hole. *Thank you, Sister Squash, for growing into such plump and delicious food for us to eat. We honor you by planting you next to Sister Corn and Sister Bean and watering your seeds.* Cover up the seeds and pour water on the hole.

Now we place a small twig in the ground to mark where we have planted the seeds so we will know where to water them every day.

All: *Grow together our Three Sisters, be happy and grow together. May all the seeds in our garden grow and be happy. We bless you and ask the Great Spirit to send sun and rain to help you grow and we are thankful to take care of you and share your bounty. And, so it is.*

Plant the rest of the Three Sisters seeds and the rest of the garden.

Note: This ceremony can also be performed for gardens planted in pots.

BLESSING OF THE RIVERS, PONDS, AND LAKES

Water is the symbol of the sacred life-blood of Mother Earth. The rivers, ponds and lakes represent that life-giving substance and it is important for us to bless them. Blessing the water changes the energy of the water and enhances its ability to heal. This blessing ceremony has been done by the Grandmothers of the Shining Valley in our community. In many Native American traditions, women are responsible for the water. The Grandmothers especially feel a deep responsibility to bless and keep the water clean to heal all of Creation. This ceremony is more meaningful when done at the bank of the river or on the shores of the pond or lake and the grandmothers of the community are invited to participate. The Grandmothers hold the heart and the wisdom of the water.

Supplies: Rose petals in a basket.

Instructions: Gather on a good day on the edge of a river, lake or pond. (If there are several bodies of water, choose the most convenient). Invite the community to the ceremony in advance. This ceremony is best held close to the spring equinox or on the summer solstice. Have the rose petals in the basket ready to be used in the ceremony.

Opening

Leader: Thank you, grandmothers and all the women, and the men for being here to bless our river. The river is the heart of our community. It provides us with water, recreation and beauty. It flows through our community creating habitats for the fish, birds and animals. Plants and trees grow along its banks and our families play in its cooling waters. This river is the lifeblood of Mother Earth that nourishes our life in this place. It is a sacred gift from the Creator.

Leader may step into the water and lift up a handful for this prayer. Let us pray: *Great Spirit, we give thanks for the waters of life that flow through our homes. We give thanks for the oceans, the clouds and the skies that continue to fill the life of our river. We ask your blessings on this river and on this community, that we may flow together in peace for the good of all life. And, so it is.*

We invite the Grandmothers to come forward first to take a few rose petals in their hands, hold them close to their hearts, and put a blessing in them, take them to the water and scattered them. The river will take our blessings out into the world. (Help Grandmothers to the river to scatter petals.) The women will come next and then the men. (Help anyone who needs a hand.)

Leader: *Bless us Sacred Spirit and bless our river as it takes our blessings out into the world. We honor the heart of our community as we honor You, O Spirit, as the heart of our lives. And, so it is.*

BLESSING THE BOATS

The Blessing of the Boats was brought to America by the many immigrants who came to the coastal lands. The original purpose was to bless the boats to help protect the sailors who made their living from the sea. These blessing ceremonies are still held in many coastal towns. Many boat owners, boat clubs, and boat communities also have blessing ceremonies for their boats today. The ceremony is usually held before the fishing season or as the weather turns good for sailing. Each boat is sprinkled with holy water.

Supplies: Pure water that has been blessed, enough to bless all the participating boats; appropriate music; special readings. ("Blessing of the Boats" by Lucille Clifton is a popular poem to read.) (Readings from the Bible are also popular.)

Instructions: Inform people in advance that there will be a Blessing of the Boats ceremony with date and time. A good time is 10-11 am. Set up a sound system, if needed.

Opening

Leader: We are gathered this beautiful day to bless these boats and all those who sail in them. Blessing of the Fleet has a long and deeply meaningful history for those who make their living from the sea. The ceremony has grown to include all those who love the oceans and waters of our great Mother Earth. We not only ask blessings for the boats and the sailors but for all the creatures who live in the sea, for the sand, the ocean plants, the coral reefs, the whales, and dolphins, and the tiny creatures who are a part of our nourishing food chain. We also bless the sea birds who sustain the harmony of the waters.

Let us pray: *Great Spirit of the Divine who holds the waters of the Earth in your hands, bless these boats and the men and women who work and travel on them. Protect them and bring them safely home. Bless all those throughout the world and throughout the ages who have lost their lives at sea and especially those whose families live with our families in this community.*

May we always care for the sea and our environment with respect and may we honor the place the sea has in all our lives, not only for the food it gives to our bodies, but also for the beauty it gives to our hearts. Our oceans have been here since the beginning of time nurturing the beginnings of life and they continue to nurture us. We are all children of the sea. Thank you, O Great Spirit, for this gift of the seas. Thank you for our life and all our blessings that come from the sea. And, so it is.

The owners of the boats may now step forward, and together we will bless each boat. As we sprinkle each boat with holy water, please add your own blessings for your beloved craft.

(Go around to each boat in the harbor in a prayerful manner.) *Bless you in the name of the Holy Spirit of the Sea. Sail swiftly and safely into the waters of the sea, carrying our blessings to all of life. And, so it is.*

Changing of the Seasons

CHANGING OF THE
SEASONS CEREMONIES

※

Traditional cultures celebrate the changing of the seasons to honor the Great Circle of Life and our part in it. When we are mindful, we too can feel the changes of the seasons "in our bones." Performing ceremonies at these times deepens our understanding of change in our lives. It brings forth a spiritual awareness of change. The constant change in our lives is not to be feared but honored and revered. It is also important for children to have the experience of welcoming change, so their lives will unfold in a gentle way knowing their place in creation.

These ceremonies for the Changing of the Seasons are held outdoors, at home, in a park, or around a Peace Pole. They provide an opportunity for participants to reflect on the positive aspects of each season and the beauty each one brings for growth. The ceremonies are also times to pray for the healing of our Mother the Earth and for peace.

The spring equinox (March 21) and the fall equinox (September 21) were celebrated by our ancestors as special times of balance and harmony when the Light and the Dark, day and night, were equal. It is a powerful time and prayers said within this balance are more powerful. The summer solstice (June 21) celebrates the longest day of the year and all the blessings that Light can bring. The winter solstice (December 21) celebrates the longest night of the year and is a time of hope, to remember that the Light will come again. The solstices are also powerful times. We take these opportunities for self-healing and for sending out prayers for the healing of the world, for peace and understanding.

The Prayers to the Four Directions included with each of these special ceremonies are found in the Appendix. (Check online for the exact times of the equinoxes and solstices if you want to do a ritual at the exact time of change.)

SPRING EQUINOX GATHERING

The spring equinox is celebrated on March 21. It is the traditional beginning of the year for our ancestors and for those who live close to the land. It is the time of preparing and planting, of awakening, of hope and planning for the future.

Supplies: Drums; seeds to share, placed in the center of the circle; sage for smudging.

Instructions: Participants smudge before coming into the circle, (optional). Form a circle and play the drums until the energy lifts and becomes harmonious, or sing a special spring song. Say the prayers to the Four Directions, then allow all participants to share their prayers for spring, peace, and the healing of Mother Earth. Bless the seeds. Drum again to send the prayers. The ceremony ends with a circle dance or drum round and a prayer. Participants share the seeds they brought to be taken home and planted.

Opening

Leader: Let us drum the heartbeat of Mother Earth as we prepare this circle for our sacred prayers. (Drumming until the Leader feels the energy shift to harmony.) The Earth is changing from winter to spring. The days are longer now. and the sun is returning to its new position in the East. New life is stirring in the ground and the baby animals are being born in the pastures. The trees are growing their green coats and the wind is singing of warmer days to come. It is the time of the Spring Equinox, when the day and the night are equal. It is a time for planting gardens and a time to plant new ideas in our lives. It is time to bring ourselves back to balance and harmony, to release what has frozen us in the past, and plant new seeds of joy and abundance.

Prayer for Peace

Leader: *O Great Spirit of our Ancestors, I raise my pipe to you, to your messengers the four winds, and to Mother Earth who provides for your children. Give us the wisdom to teach our children to love, to respect, and to be kind to each other so that they may grow with peace in mind. Let us learn to share all the good things that you provide for us on this Earth. May we be mindful of what we plant in thought, word and deed, so our children unto the Seventh Generation may live in peace and harmony. Aho.*

Prayers to the Four Directions

We open with prayers to the Four Directions and the Center which symbolize the wholeness of the circle we stand in here today. (Prayers to the Four Directions are found in the Appendix or you may create your own.)

Sharing

Since spring is the time for new beginnings for the Earth, you are invited to share your prayers for new beginnings. Prayers for the healing of Mother Earth and for peace in the world are also welcome.

Closing

Let us seal our prayers with the Circle Dance of the Native Americans. As you take each step envision healing going down into Mother Earth and the energy of Peace beginning to move through this circle and out into the world.

Dance: Moving clockwise, take a sidestep with the left foot. Bring the right foot next to it as a touch, then step with the left foot again, moving around the circle. Bend the knees slightly as the steps are taken. Drummers may accompany the dance with a 4/4 beat. Dance around the circle one time.

Closing Prayer

Leader: *Spirits of the East, South, West and North, we release you now with gratitude that you are always with us. Hear this closing prayer from the Sioux Nation:*

> Grandfather Great Spirit,
> All over the world the faces of living ones are alike.
> With tenderness they have come up out of the ground
> Look upon your children that they may face the winds
> And walk the good road to the Day of Quiet.
> Grandfather Great Spirit
> Fill us with the Light.
> Give us the strength to understand, and the eyes to see.
> Teach us to walk the soft Earth as relatives to all that live. Aho.

Participants share the seeds they brought.

SUMMER SOLSTICE GATHERING

June 21st marks the Summer Solstice, when the Earth experiences the longest day in the year. It is the time of fullness as the plants and animals are ripening, blossoming, and maturing. The joy of life abounds everywhere. People are friendlier, families get together, and life feels good. Summer is also the time for nurturing the seeds we planted in our lives in spring. We are responsible to care for our seed-ideas to help them grow and blossom. They will bring us great power in this time of fulfillment of summer. If we do not take time to water and tend our seed-ideas, they will wither and die.

Supplies: Drums; cornmeal in a small bowl; sage for smudging, lighter.

Instructions: Participants smudge with the sacred smoke of the sage before entering the circle. Form a circle and play the drums until the energy lifts and moves into harmony or sing a special song. Prayers to the Four Directions are said then participants are invited to share their prayers for summer, peace, and the healing of Mother Earth. Bless the cornmeal. The ceremony ends with a circle dance or drum round and a prayer. Participants share a bit of cornmeal with a nearby plant as a symbol of the act of nurturing.

Opening

Leader: Let us drum the heartbeat of Mother Earth. (When Leader feels the energy shift, he/she begins) This is the midpoint of the year – the time to reflect on our progress towards fulfilling our promises to live in peace and our prayers for change we made at the spring equinox. Living in peace means first being at peace in our hearts, then living in peace in our families, with our neighbors, in our community, in our nation, and in the world. Living in peace means accepting all our sisters and brothers of every faith or no faith, for each path has a part of the Truth.

Summer is also a time to reflect on what we have been doing to nurture our new ideas and the new way we wish to live upon the earth. Our prayers today will bless this cornmeal, a symbol of sustenance. At the end of the gathering, we will each take a small portion and offer it to a nearby bush or tree as a re-affirmation of our desire to continue to nourish our dreams.

Prayer for Peace

Leader: *O, Great Spirit who dwells in the sky, lead us to the path of peace and understanding. Let all of us live together as brothers and sisters. Our lives are so short here, walking on Mother Earth's surface, let our eyes be opened to all the blessings you have given us. Please hear our prayers. Aho.*

Prayers to the Four Directions

We begin our ceremony with prayers to the Four Directions. (See Appendix)

Sharing

Summer is the time of Light, the time of dancing and joy. It is a time to remember that we are one with all Creation, from the tiny insect to the great whale. It is a time to remember we are a part of the great web of life and that what happens to even a tiny part of the web happens to us. This the time for sharing our prayers, especially our prayers for peace and the healing of Mother Earth. (Share prayers)

Closing

Let us seal our prayers with the Circle Dance of the Native Americans. As you take each step envision healing going down into Mother Earth and the energy of Peace beginning to move through this circle and out into the world.

Dance: Moving clockwise, take a sidestep with the left foot. Bring the right foot next to it as a touch, then step with the left foot again, moving around the circle. Bend the knees slight as the steps are taken. Drummers may accompany the dance with a 4/4 beat. Dance around the circle one time.

Closing Prayer

Leader: *Spirits of the East, South, West and North, we release you now with gratitude that you are always with us. Help me remember to never take more than I need and to always give back more than I take. Aho.*

Participants take a small measure of the cornmeal and offer it to a nearby bush or tree as a blessing and reminder of the importance of nurturing our dreams.

AUTUMN EQUINOX GATHERING

This the time of balance, the second time during the year that the day and the night are equal. It is the time to honor the Autumn Equinox, September 21. Balance is a gift and one we should not take lightly. Balance allows us to live on the straight path in harmony with both the physical and the spiritual world. The vertical line is the path of Spirit. The horizontal line is the path of the Earth. We stand where the two paths intersect, in this present moment.

Supplies: Drums: colorful autumn leaves; sage for smudging, lighter.

Instructions: Participants smudge with the sacred smoke of the sage before entering the circle. Form a circle and play the drums until the energy lifts and moves into harmony, or sing a special song. Prayers to the Four Directions are said, then participants share their prayers for autumn, peace, and the healing of Mother Earth. The ceremony ends with a circle dance or drumming round and a prayer.

Opening

Leader: Let us drum the heartbeat of Mother Earth. (When Leader feels the energy shift, he/she begins.)

The Autumn Equinox reminds us that what we have sown, so shall we reap. If we planted seeds of kindness and compassion in the spring, we will reap the fruits of those seeds here in the Autumn. This is the time to inspire, awaken, uplift, and heal our lives with a fuller understanding of our spiritual lives

Prayer for Peace

O, Eagle, come with wings outspread in sunny skies. O, Eagle, come and bring us peace, thy gentle peace. O, Eagle, come and give new life to us who pray. Remember the circle of the sky, the stars, and the brown eagle, the great life of the Sun, the young within the nest. Remember the sacredness of all things. Aho. – Pawnee Prayer.

Prayers to the Four Directions

We begin our ceremony with prayers to the Four Directions. (See Appendix)

Sharing

This is the time of the gathering of the harvest, a time to be thankful for the abundance of the crops and for enough food to survive the cold of Winter. In the early days of our European ancestors, the harvests of the vine, wine and apples and the harvest of the hunt were celebrated. In the Americas, the celebration centered around corn and the other staples of life.

Half is Day, Half is night.
Harvest Moon. Golden Bright.
Spiral out and spiral in.
Harvest, death, rebirth again. (Wiccan)

This the time for sharing our prayers, especially our prayers for peace and the healing of Mother Earth. Our prayers will also bless these autumn leaves whose beauty is the beauty of our dreams fulfilled. (Share prayers)

Closing

Let us seal our prayers with the Circle Dance of the Native Americans. As you take each step envision healing going down into Mother Earth and the energy of Peace beginning to move through this circle and out into the world.

Dance: Moving clockwise, take a sidestep with the left foot. Bring the right foot next to it as a touch, then step with the left foot again, moving around the circle. Bend the knees slight as the steps are taken. Drummers may accompany the dance with a 4/4 beat. Dance around the circle one time.

Closing Prayer

Leader: *Spirits of the East, South, West and North, we release you now with gratitude that you are always with us.* Hear this closing prayer from the Chinook people of the Northwest.

May all I say and all I think be in harmony with thee, God within me, God beyond me, maker of the trees. Aho.

Participants are invited to take a leaf home with them to remind them of the beauty of God in every season.

WINTER SOLSTICE GATHERING

The Winter Solstice, December 21, falls in the middle of the end-of-year celebrations. This is the time when the day is the shortest and the night the longest in the Western Hemisphere. Our ancient ancestors built huge bonfires on the hills above the villages and kept watch all night to greet the rising sun with thanksgiving – praising the Gods that the sun did return. This time of year, we call for peace to spread over the earth with goodwill for all. It is a time of remembrance and a time to brighten our homes and lives before the cold contemplative time of winter sets in.

In 2012 at the time of the Winter Solstice, the sun rose up directly into the center of our galaxy forming the vertical pole of a great cross. Our solar system moved into position as the horizontal bar. The Earth is at the end of a cosmic cycle of 26,000 years. The world's prophecies foretold of a time of turmoil followed by a Golden Age when humanity would live together in peace. It is up to each of us to do our part to bring humanity into the Golden Age of Peace.

Supplies: Drums; evergreen boughs; sage for smudging, lighter.

Instructions: Participants smudge with the sacred smoke of the sage before entering the circle. Form a circle and play the drums until the energy lifts and moves into harmony, or a special winter song may be sung. Prayers to the Four Directions are offered and participants share their prayers for winter, peace, and the healing of Mother Earth. Bless the evergreens. The ceremony ends with a circle dance or drum round and a prayer.

Opening

Leader: Let us drum the heartbeat of Mother Earth. (When Leader feels the energy shift, he/she begins)

On the Winter Solstice the day is the shortest and the night the longest of the year. It is a time to reflect about the darkness and what happens in the dark of our souls. Will we find fear in the Darkness or will we find the potential for possibilities? What will you find on this longest night of the year? It is also the time for healing. We heal best in the quietness and solitude.

Prayer for Peace

This is the time for healing. Our Mother the Earth needs time to heal. Our Father the Sky needs time to heal. All creatures that walk upon the Earth need time to heal. Humans need time to heal. The Great Spirit has given us this time of winter to heal when the world is peaceful and quiet and locked in serenity. This is the healing time. This is the healing time. May you be healed in body, mind, and heart. This is the time for healing and for peace.

Prayers to the Four Directions

We begin our ceremony with prayers to the Four Directions. (See Appendix)

Sharing

Leader: This the time for sharing our prayers, especially our prayers for peace and the healing of Mother Earth. (Share prayers) Our prayers will also bless these evergreen boughs which remind us of the green of spring, the hope for the future that we begin to create here in the wintertime.

(Participants are invited to take a spring of evergreen home to decorate their houses.)

Closing

Let us seal our prayers with the Circle Dance of the Native Americans. As you take each step envision healing going down into Mother Earth and the energy of Peace beginning to move through this circle and out into the world.

Dance: Moving clockwise, take a sidestep with the left foot. Bring the right foot next to it as a touch, then step with the left foot again, moving around the circle. Bend the knees slight as the steps are taken. Drummers may accompany the dance with a 4/4 beat. Dance around the circle one time.

Closing Prayer

Leader: *Spirits of the East, South, West and North, we release you now with gratitude that you are always with us.* Hear this closing prayer:

> *Creator, Great Spirit, hear our prayers as we re-dedicate ourselves today to work for peace and harmony that we may walk in beauty on our Mother the Earth. Remind us always that peace does not mean to be in a place where there is no noise, trouble or hard work. Peace means to be in the midst of those things and be calm in our heart. We promise to do everything we can to bring Mother Earth back into balance in our everyday thoughts, words and actions. We make this promise with hearts full of gratitude for the blessings you bestow upon us. Thank you, Great Spirit, for being Father-Mother-God for us, your children. Thank you for bringing peace to our hearts. Thank you for the gifts of Mother Earth. Aho.*

Ceremonies for Holidays

CEREMONIES FOR THE HOLIDAYS

Holidays are particularly good times for ceremonies. Families and friends come together to enjoy family traditions. These holiday ceremonies are based on the spiritual symbolism and meaning of the holiday. Any meaningful family tradition can be turned into a more formal ceremony. Remember that ceremonies speak to the heart and soul and may open you to a new spiritual dimension.

FIRST FOOTER RITUAL

In Scotland and other Celtic regions, the first person to step across your threshold in the new year is responsible for the luck of the family for the coming year. The family is free to call upon this person to complain about the lack of luck or to give thanks for all the good luck. As soon as the person steps across the threshold, he or she is given a gift and informed of his/her new responsibility to the family for the coming year.

NEW YEAR'S - BURNING BOWL CEREMONY

The New Year is a time for new beginnings, a time to release what hasn't served us in the past and to embrace that which we desire to become in the present and future. At the new year we are ready for healing to come into our lives. We are ready to release all the old beliefs, habits, attitudes, feelings, situations, and memories about ourselves and the world we choose to change. We embrace a new way of thinking, believing, feeling, speaking, and doing. This ceremony is an outward symbol of what we want to do within. It is a sacred way to help us start the new year in a new way.

The first step is to forgive all the old hurts done to us and ask forgiveness for all the hurts we have done to others, including ourselves. (See the Ho'oponopono Service of Forgiveness which can be done prior to the Burning Bowl ceremony.)

The Burning Bowl ceremony can be done as a family or in a community setting. It can also be done by an individual. You are encouraged to take this ceremony seriously with reverence.

Supplies: Two different colored pieces of paper and pens; a candle and lighter; a safe place to burn the papers (grill, old pan, container of sand).

Instructions: Light the candle and prepare the safe burning space. Provide one piece of paper and pen to participants. Have someone stand by the candle and fire space to make sure everyone is safe. When everyone has burned their papers, blow out the candle and set the ashes in water. After participants have burned their papers, they will go to the blessing table where the second piece of paper and pen are ready. Here they write out three blessings they want to see in their lives for the new year. Fold it and place it in the Blessing Bowl or Jar. They will be saved and returned to the owners at next year's Burning Bowl ceremony or they may take them home to put in a safe place to bring out and read next year.

Opening

Leader: We are gathered here to participate in the Burning Bowl ceremony to symbolically release all the old patterns and beliefs of our past and begin the new year with the Truth about who we are and to claim that Truth.

Let us pray: *Heavenly Father, Mother, God, we come before you now cleansed of old hurts, forgiven by You and ourselves, ready to release old patterns and beliefs about who we are. We remember with all our heart, mind and soul that we are co-creators with you and as co-creators have a responsibility to create this world anew with peace, hope, love and joy. Let your Spirit permeate every moment of our lives in this New Year as we take up the Mantle of Love to enfold ourselves, our families, our friends and all beings in the true expression of that Divine Love. Guide us in recognizing what we are to release and what we are to accept and embrace about our true nature in this new time. We are ready to start our new chapter, to co-create our new life. Thank you for your guidance and most of all for your eternal and unconditional Love. Amen. And, so it.*

Leader: Let us take some time in meditation to think about what you want to release from the past and what you want to come into your life for the new year. When you are ready, write what you want to release on a piece of paper, fold it in half and take it to the candle. In a sacred manner, light the paper on fire from the candle and place it in the Burning Bowl. Stay until it has been completely consumed by the fire. Visualize a Violet Flame burning and transforming your old beliefs as you release them to the fire.

Then go to the Blessing Table where you may write down up to three blessings that you wish to invite into your life for this New Year. Fold the paper and put it into the Blessing Jar. We will save all the blessings until next year's ceremony when you can reclaim your paper and see how many blessings came into your life. You may also take your blessings home with you to put in a safe place until next year's ceremony.

The Sufi poet, Rumi, said, "There is a place where words are born of silence; A place where the whispers of the heart arise." Let us be in the silence of our own hearts.

(Music plays as people go to burn their papers)

We seal this ceremony with this prayer: *O Creator of All Life, we come before you with gratitude in our hearts for this opportunity to make right, to transform, and to know the Truth. May we always live in harmony, peace, and love.* And, so it is.

WHITE STONE CEREMONY

The White Stone Ceremony is another ceremony for the new year. It could also be done in the spring at the beginning of the Seasons. Any kind of white stones can be used. They represent a clean slate for a new life. In ancient times, according to the Jerusalem Stone Company, which provides white stones for this ceremony, in biblical times a white stone was given to a person released from prison or released from bondage as a symbol of new life.

The white stone also represents the infinite possibilities to create the kind of future you wish. When you write your power word on the stone, it is a reminder that you have mindfully called into your present life, the thing you have written on the stone. Words have power. The more you write and speak them, the more powerful they become. When you focus on the essence of the word, and visualize that coming into your life, the more it will manifest.

Supplies: A simple altar set with 2 candles; enough white stones in a special basket for all participants; marking pens.

Instructions: Bless the stones as a group; give one stone and a marking pen to each person. At the appropriate time during the ceremony, each person will write a new name, a desire, or word of inspiration for the new year.

Opening

Leader: We are gathered today to spend some time in meditation and contemplation and to write an inspiration on our white stones symbolizing our prayers for the new year. You may want to write a new spiritual name for yourself, a deep held desire, or a spiritual goal you want to work toward. The white color of the stone represents a clean slate, a fresh start, and purity. All new desires begin with purity of spirit, purity of desire, purity of manifestation. The stone represents bringing the desire into solid form, one you can experience with all your senses.

Let us pray: *Divine Mystery of All Life, Holy Spirit, be with us as we reach deep into our souls to find our path for this new year. May this new inspiration be sacred and holy to our lives. May we move forward with joy and anticipation that this new inspiration will manifest within and may we express it outwardly. May this new activity be one that bring heart and mind and soul into new alignment and may we be guided to our sacred purpose of love. And, so it is.*

Holding your white stone in your hands, take four deep breaths, breathing in Light and breathing out Peace. When you have reached your deep Center of Peace, allow your heart to open to the higher White Stone consciousness. Become one with all that is in this place of sacred peace.

This is the deep space of unlimited possibilities, of becoming our full potential, of realizing the God within you. Relax into this space opening your heart fully to the sacred wisdom of your soul. Continue breathing in a relaxed way. Invite the activity of God into your heart and mind for the next few minutes. Focus on being receptive to hearing the voice of God through your soul.

Stay in this peace until your soul speaks to you with a holy word that you can write on your white stone. What are you being guided to do in this new year? What quality of spirit does your soul want you to express for your higher good? Do you need a new spiritual name that better describes your vibrational energy? Be open to what comes. Do not force the inspiration. Stay relaxed and expectant. The inspiration may come as an actual word that you hear, an impression or a feeling. Continue to be at peace and wait.

When you have received your inspiration to write on your White Stone, repeat it three times and then write it on your stone. Continue to hold your stone in your hands meditating on your inspiration until everyone has written on their stones.

Take another deep breath now and join in this blessing: *I bless this stone and ask that it holds my inspiration for the new year. Let the power of the alignment of my heart, mind and soul guide me to a better expression of who I really am. I am a Light Worker, bringing Light to all I meet. Let this inspiration increase the Light of who I am and what I give. And so it is.*

Closing

Let us close with a blessing for all the White Stones. Please bring your stone with you, place it on the altar and join in the circle.

Blessing: As we place these stones into the Circle let the inspirations written upon them become the strength of our community (family), to fulfill our purpose of peace and compassion. We bless each stone and the person who carries it with the love and light of the Divine.

Accept this consciousness of the ever increasing good in your life and carry this white stone as a reminder of what you have chosen to do in this new year. Our prayers have taken flight, let the rain of blessings flow. And, so it is.

Sing a peace song for the closing.

EASTER CEREMONY OF RENEWAL
MEDITATION AND DANCE

Many religions celebrate rebirth and renewal at the Spring Equinox. This is the New Year Celebration for many cultures. Renewal traditions have been passed on from one generation to the next from ancient times to modern times, from older religions to newer ones. These traditions center around rebirth, death and resurrection.

In Christianity, Easter is the time to celebrate the resurrection of Jesus the Christ. In ancient Germany, the Goddess Ostara was celebrated as she became pregnant at the Spring Equinox in anticipation of the birth of the Light or the Sun God on the Winter Solstice. In ancient Saxony, Eostre, whose name means spring, was celebrated on the first full moon after the Spring Equinox (the same date as Easter is celebrated today). She was rescued by her pet bird in the cold of winter and during the rescue the bird's wings were frozen. To save the bird, Eostre transformed it into a rabbit. The transformation wasn't complete though and the rabbit retained the ability to lay eggs. That is why our modern Easter Bunny brings colored eggs. We celebrate many ancient traditions in this spring renewal ceremony.

Supplies and Set up: Chairs are set in a circle, two rows if needed. In the center is a circular table set with bright, spring cloth. Set up the candles and the Peace Candle and flowers. Bring a basket filled with eggs which have an affirmation inside. Use Easter grass and flowers to fill in.

Instructions: As people enter the Circle, they are given an egg as a symbol of renewal and asked not to open it but to hold it throughout the ceremony to add blessings to the prayers and affirmations that they contain.

Opening

Leader: Welcome to the Circle of Renewal. It is Easter and the Spring Equinox, a time of balance, a perfect time to release the reflections of winter and take the wisdom we have learned into the renewal of spring. The world is waking up again as our spirits are waking up.

Unto this darkness which is beyond Light we pray that we may come, and through loss of sight and knowledge may we see and know that which transcends sight and knowledge, and by the very fact of not seeing and knowing—we find real sight and knowledge. –Dionysius, Syria, 4th Century

Music - Easter Song of Renewal

Prayer of Renewal

Leader: Let us pray: *Holy Divine Mystery, Creator of All Life, we ask your blessings on the people gathered here who are renewed in Your Love. Guide us to look at the world through new eyes and listen to the songs of spring with new ears. We celebrate the return of the daylight, new growth, and new inspiration. Thank you for all the blessings you have given us and for the all the blessings to come. And, so it is.*

CIRCLE MEDITATION

Leader: We are all connected in the great Circle of Life and we especially sense this in springtime. Our hearts and spirits reach out to embrace the new life growing all around us. We feel renewed. To experience this renewing connection, we will do a special meditation.

I invite you now to close your eyes and take a deep breath. Gently relax your body, your emotions and your mind. Take another deep breath and move your consciousness to that place just behind your heart where the flame of Spirit burns within you. Feel yourself in that Center of Peace. Take another deep breath and now open your spiritual eyes and see yourself in this circle. You are part of this circle… you are the circle…close your eyes again.

Reach out with your spirit hands and take the spirit hand of the person on each side of you and feel the collective Love of all the people who are together in this circle…breathe together for a few moments strengthening this bond of Love.

As you breathe together you realize that you breathe with all of creation…especially with all of creation on Mother Earth…you feel spiritual roots begin to travel down from your feet…into the ground, reaching down into the earth…connecting you with our Great Mother. Mother Earth welcomes you and gives you renewing energy that nourishes and sustains you and you feel it returning up through your spiritual roots…up through your feet, up your legs and up through your spine. This renewing energy travels up to your heart, out through your arms and around the Circle. You share this energy with everyone in this circle, passing it out through your left hand and receiving it with your right… and you breathe this energy with Mother Earth and with all her children here in this Circle. Breathe this energy around and around the Circle.

Now as you receive this loving energy through your right hand you direct it upward to your crown where it joins with your Divine energy and is transformed into Light. You direct this transformed energy down to your heart and out your left hand to the person on your left. Breathe slowly and continue to receive this energy with your right hand, lift it to your crown, transform it into Light and pass it on through your left hand.

The Circle glows brighter with the Light of the Divine, each segment transformed and beautified by each Divine Spark of Life in the Circle. This Circle is a blazing Light here in this community. Now send this energy and your prayers for Peace and Renewal out into the world like ripples from a pebble dropped in a pool of water. Each ripple will travel miles and miles until the whole world is awash in Light. Keep sending out peace and light on your breath…sending out peace and light on your breath.

Now take another deep breath and let the last ripple go and bring your consciousness back to the Circle. Release the Light and return to your Heart Center. Say a prayer of thanksgiving for this Light…for this Love…for this Circle…Know that you are forever a part of the Great Circle of Light and you can join this Circle of Light at any time to share your own Divine Light and peace with the world.

Take another deep breath and begin to feel the chair underneath you. Wiggle your toes and fingers and when you are ready, open your eyes and feel whole, complete and perfect…renewed in heart, mind, spirit and body on this beautiful Easter morning. 1-2-3 eyes open, wide awake.

Dance of Renewal

Leader: Take your egg with you as we form a double circle for the Dance of Renewal. When the circle is complete. take a deep breath and open the egg. Read the message inside two times to yourself. This message is for you and for someone else in the circle. Return the message to the egg and hold it in readiness for the dance.

This is a simple dance. Stand in front of a partner. The people in the inside circle place the egg in their left hand. The people in the outside circle place the egg in their right hand. Repeat the words as you do the dance movements.

I am the Light – hold egg in front of your heart

You are the Light – give egg to partner (exchange eggs)

We are the Light – turn in a circle in place to the right

That will change the world – turn a circle in place to the left

Inside circle moves one partner to the right and repeat until the eggs have been exchanged many times. The right message will end up in the hands of the person who is meant to receive it.

When the dance is over, everyone opens their eggs and reads their special message.

Closing Prayer

Leader: *Thank you, Holy Spirit, for the gift of these inspirations. We will read them often to remind us of Your Love in this time of renewal. May all the world be at Peace and filled with Light. And, so it is.*

MESSENGERS OF LIGHT CEREMONY

This is a favorite of our spiritual community as it honors all the messengers from all the religions in one ceremony. It is a good ceremony to do on Christmas Eve or for New Year's. The ceremony includes readings from different religions and special music to be played or sung before each religion is honored. (We use a combination of CD's and group songs) This ceremony can be lengthened into a full church service.

Supplies and Set Up: Symbols representing all the religion are set up on two long tables covered with white clothes; a votive candle is set in front of each symbol; 2 lighters; garlands or greenery placed along the back of the symbols for decoration; two adult readers and one child reader; two candle lighters. The symbols are set so that the candles will be lighted from each table alternately from outside to inside. (Check the ceremony to determine the setup of the symbols and candles.) Oil in a small bowl for the Blessing of the Children. You will also need music for each religion.

Instructions: The two candle lighters will alternately light the votive candles as the reading for that religion begins. Music for the religion is played or sung before the readings. Suggested music is included with the ceremony, but you may choose other appropriate music. The Blessing of the Children follows the candle lighting ceremony.

Opening

Leader: And God said, "Let there be light; and there was light. And God saw that the light was good." (Genesis1:3-4) The Messengers of Light, the wise sages, the prophets, the great teachers of every spiritual path, are sent by the Divine Power that is known by many names, to remind us that we are the Children of the Light, the Children of Love. Their message has been told since the beginning of time.

And they came, each out of the darkness of their own time, mantled in physical form, to bring the Light to the people. Some were shunned, some were killed, some died a natural death, but the Light they brought into the world will never be extinguished. These are the Messengers of Light from ages past and for our own times. Other Messengers of Light are still to come in the future and our hope is that humanity will see the Light within them and awaken into a new world filled with Love and Peace.

A great modern Light Bringer said, *"There has never been a time on Earth like we see today. What we need are more ways to experience our interconnectedness - it is a precursor to deep love. So, in this quickening light, with the dawn of each new day, let us look for love. Let us no longer struggle. Let us ever become who we most want to be. As we begin to be who we truly are, the world will be a better place."* -- John Denver

We celebrate the Messengers of Light and their Messages of Love and Peace by lighting our twelve candles and listening to their teachings. At the end of the service we invite you to come forward for the Blessing of the Children, as we are all Children of the Light. We celebrate the Light with our ancestors, our families, our friends, all our relations on the Earth, and with our children, for they are symbols of that Holy and Sacred Light that God called into the world and saw that it was good.

Let us pray: *O Creator of All Life, we give thanks this beautiful morning (evening) for the Light that is reborn in our hearts, our families and the world. We pray that the true message of peace on earth and goodwill towards each other will be heard. Bless all of the followers of the Messengers of the Light as we renew our faith and lift our spirits. Bless all those who work for peace and compassion. And, so it is!*

"I have come to light the lamp of love in your hearts, to see that it shines day by day with added luster." -- Sai Baba

UNIVERSAL BEGINNINGS - THE GODDESS

READER #1 - <u>Honoring the Goddess:</u> "Queen of Winter, Mother of All, hear us as our voices call. Send your fire back to earth, as we will the Sun's rebirth. As the flames around us glow, so may love within us grow." – Wiccan Prayer to the Goddess

Reader #1 - We light the First Candle in honor of Our Great Mother, the Goddess, the Birther of the Light. Our Great Mother has many names, among them, Gaia and Kwan Lin, Shanti and Mary. The Great Mother nourishes our bodies and our souls. She brings forth the Light from the darkness of her womb and shows us the wisdom of the heart. Her great compassion was revered by all our ancient ancestors. The Goddess teaches us about the cycles of life, of birth and death, and our part in those cycles. She teaches us to cultivate and harvest, to take care of everyone and everything, for each part of creation is a sacred gift. The Goddess teaches us how to listen to the intuition in our hearts, to follow the path of inclusiveness, and to share with each other. We light this candle in Her Honor, in honor of the Wiccan and Pagan people, and all the earth-based traditional faiths and in honor of all women, who are her living symbols.

TRADITIONAL - NATIVE AMERICAN

READER #1 - <u>Honoring White Buffalo Calf Woman:</u> "You will walk like a living prayer with your feet resting upon the earth. Your body forms a living bridge between the Sacred Beneath and the Sacred Above. Wakan Tanka smiles upon us, because now we are as one: earth, sky, all living things, the two-legged, the four-legged, the winged ones, the finned-ones, the trees, the grasses. Together with the people, they are all related, one family." – Wisdom of White Buffalo Calf Woman

READER #2 - We light the Second Candle for White Buffalo Calf Woman who came to the Lakota people and for all the Shamans around the world, who were the Messengers of Light for our ancestors and for all the traditional paths today. They taught the First People to live close to our Mother the Earth; to care for the living land and the animals and take only what they needed so that all Beings could live in peace and harmony. These Messengers of the Great Spirit teach us how to live with all our relations on earth, to respect the sacred, and to walk in beauty. They teach us that our most important connection is our personal connection with the Creator. We light this candle in their honor and in honor of all Medicine Men and Women who carry the sacred bundles of the first Nations for all the people of Mother Earth.

AKHENATON OF EGYPT

READER #1 - <u>Honoring Akhenaton:</u> "Splendid you rise, O living Aten, eternal Lord! You are radiant, beauteous, mighty. Your love is great, immense, your rays light up all faces, your bright hue gives life to hearts. All peoples, herds, and flocks, all trees that grow from soil, they live when you dawn for them. You are mother and father of all that you made." -- Prayer to the Sun God of Ancient Egypt

READER #2 - The Third Candle honors the Aten and his Messenger of Light, Akhenaton, Pharaoh of all Egypt, the Son of Light, who taught us that the Love of God shines down upon us eternally through the Great Sun that rises every morning and brings Light, warmth and nourishment into our lives. He taught us to be thankful for the goodness and bounty of life and to be thankful for all our blessings. We light this candle in honor of Akhenaton, who had the courage to stand up for One God, and in honor of all rulers and leaders of the people in every land today who are caretakers of their people and we pray that they use their power for the highest good of all to bring peace and light unto their lands.

HINDU - LORD KRISHNA OF INDIA

READER #1 - <u>Honoring Lord Krishna:</u> "High hath the Mighty risen before the dawning, and come to us with light out of the darkness. Thou, being born, art Child of Earth and Heaven...to

the Gods' pathway have we traveled, ready to execute what work we may accomplish."—Prayer to Lord Krishna

READER #2 - The Fourth Candle honors Lord Krishna of the Hindu faith, who came to show us that the darkness is always overcome by the Light and that we can be spiritual and still live in the physical world. We honor Lord Krishna with this candle and honor all the Hindu people who teach us to celebrate with great joy, to illuminate our lives with thousands of candles that reflect the great love of God, the Atman, and to realize that the waters of the Earth are sacred. We light this candle for all the people of the world, who are all the children of the Earth and children of the waters.

JUDAISM - ABRAHAM AND MOSES

READER #1- <u>Honoring Abraham and Moses:</u> And the Angel of the Lord said to Abraham, "The Lord says that because you obeyed me and have not withheld your only son from me, I will bless you and your seed shall be as the stars of the heaven and the sand which is upon the sea shore and in thy seed shall all the nations of the earth be blessed." – The Torah, the Old Testament of the Bible

READER #2 - The Fifth Candle honors Abraham, the Great Father of the Children of Israel, the Children of Islam and the Children of Christianity, who listened to God's voice and brought forth the people dedicated to the Law. Abraham taught that faith is more powerful than anything else and that faith can bring us miracles. Abraham taught that families are important and that we must love and honor each member of our family. We also honor Moses, who brought the Children of Israel out of the land of Egypt following a pillar of Light. Moses brought the Ten Commandments, a moral code to live by, from the mountain of God. We light this candle in honor of Abraham and Moses, to honor the Jewish faith, and to honor our families and those who follow their own faith to bring forth miracles.

ZOROASTRIANISM - ZOROASTER OF PERSIA

READER #1 - <u>Honoring Zoroaster:</u> "O, Ahura Mazda, when I was looking for you with my wisdom and mind and tried to find you with the eye of my heart, I recognized that you are the starter and the end of everything. You are the source of wisdom and reflection and you are the creator of truthfulness and purity and the judge and justice for the behavior of all human beings." – Prayer of Zoroaster.

READER #2 - We light the Sixth Candle in honor of Zoroaster, "He of the Golden Light," founder of the religion of the Magi of Persia, who followed Ahura Mazda, the Wise Lord. It was the Magi who found and brought gifts to the infant Jesus. Zoroaster taught us first about baptism by water and the symbolism of the communion bread, about purity and cleanliness. He taught that everyone has the liberty to choose the right way. Zoroaster honored the One God and used the symbol of fire to represent the nature of God. We honor Zoroaster and all men as we light this candle. They teach us of the Fire of the Spirit that flames within.

BUDDHISM - BUDDHA OF NEPAL

READER #1- <u>Honoring Buddha:</u> "Right views will be the torch to light his way. Right aspirations will be his guide. Right speech will be his dwelling-place on the road. His gait will be straight, for it is right behavior. His refreshments will be the right way of earning his livelihood. Right efforts will be his steps, right thoughts his breath; and right contemplation will give him the peace that follows in his footprints." – Wisdom from The Buddha.

READER #2 - We light the Seventh Candle in honor of Buddha, the Lord of Light of the Buddhist faith, who taught the Eight-Fold Path of Living. Lord Buddha taught us the importance of right mindfulness and that all beings on the earth deserve to find happiness. Buddha taught us to honor all life wherever we find it. He said that right thought and right action bring an end to our suffering and that we each have the ability to attain enlightenment. He taught us the importance of meditation and deep contemplation. We light this candle in honor of Lord Buddha, the Dalai Lama, Lao Tzu, Confucius, all the Gurus and Teachers of the other Eastern faiths that awaken us to the possibility of living a wise and compassionate life so that we may bring peace into our hearts and into the world.

CHRISTIANITY – JESUS THE CHRIST

READER #1 - <u>Honoring Jesus:</u> "I am the light of the world: he that followeth me shall not walk in darkness, but shall have the light of life." –John 8:12, King James Version of the Bible

READER #2 - The Eighth Candle is lit in honor of Jesus the Christ, the Light of the World of the Christian faith, who taught us to love God with all our being and to treat our neighbors as we would wish to be treated. It is the birth of Jesus that we celebrate at Christmas, as the Light of God born in the lowly parts of us that rises and shines in the heavens. It is the light of that great star that shown at his birth that leads us onward. Jesus taught us that there is no death and that life is everlasting. He taught us that Love is the most powerful force in the Universe and that we should always seek peace. We light this candle in honor of Jesus and all the peace makers of the world.

ISLAM – MOHAMMED THE PROPHET

READER # 1 - <u>Honoring Mohammed:</u> "He is God, the Creator, the Maker, the Fashioner. His are all the names beautiful. Whatever is in the heavens and the earth sing His praises. He is all-mighty and all-wise." – the Koran of Islam

READER #2 - We light the Ninth Candle in honor of Mohammed, the Disciple of Light of the Islam faith. Mohammed taught us that we cannot separate our daily life from our spiritual life. He taught the importance of prayers and right living. He taught about charity and to take care of and protect those who need our help. He taught us to spend time reflecting on our faith and to practice self-discipline. We light this candle in honor of Mohammed and all the prophets who remind us we are one in the Spirit of God.

BAHA'I – BAHA'U'LLAH

READER #1 - <u>Honoring Baha'u'llah:</u> "With the hands of power I made thee and with the fingers of strength I created thee; and within thee have I placed the essence of My light. Be thou content with it and seek naught else, for My work is perfect and My command is binding."– the Baha'i Prayer Book

READER #2 - The Tenth Candle honors Baha'u'llah, (Bah-ha-**oo**-lah) the Messenger of Light of the Baha'i faith, who taught us that we are one people with a common destiny and that we all live together on one world. He taught us to create resolution instead of making war on each other. He taught that everyone deserves to be treated equally and have the education we need to grow and become good stewards of the earth. He taught us that all religious paths should be respected because they all lead to the Truth and that we should give up prejudice, poverty, and wealth. He taught that one's whole life should be a prayer. We light this candle in honor of Baha'u'llah and all those who are striving to bring all people together in Unity.

THE LIGHT BEARERS

READER #1 - <u>Honoring The Light Bearers:</u> "We are that Essence of the One which expresses Divine Love, Light, Joy, Healing and Peace. We are that Extension of The One that reflects Understanding, Compassion, Empathy and Co-operation. We are the Light Bearers." –Message of the Light Bearers

READER #2 - The Eleventh Candle is for the Light Bearers, for all of us, for we are our own teachers and Messengers of Light. We teach ourselves by the choices we make, by each action we take in the name of Love, for each thought that becomes enlightened, and for each whole-hearted feeling we experience as we serve one another. We light this candle in honor of the heart and mind and soul of each one of us which contains the precious jewel of the Light of God's Love.

CHILDREN OF THE LIGHT

READER #1 – <u>Honoring the Children of Light</u>. "Your children are not your children. They are the sons and daughters of Life's longing for itself. They come through you but not from you... for their souls dwell in the house of tomorrow... You are the bows from which your children as living arrows are sent forth."– Kahlil Gibran

CHILD READER - "This is for you – I will give you my treasures I kept for a long time. I will give you a petal that falls from a rose. I will give you the first golden leaf that falls in autumn. I will give you the sunken diamond that shines more than the sun. I will give you the last treasure, the seashell that echoes like the ocean. I will give you all my treasures because I love you". – Sierra, age 8.

READER #2 - We light the Twelfth candle for the Children, the Light of our Lives, our hope for the future and a better world. Our Children teach us about unconditional love, to remember there are unlimited possibilities. They teach us how to release the old and embrace the new, to look at life from different perspectives, and to continue to dream. We honor the Children of all Beings, each child in our families, and the Child that dwells inside each of our hearts as we light the Twelfth Candle.

Blessing of the Children

Leader: We invite all the children to come forward now to receive their Blessing. And we invite everyone else to come forward to receive your blessing for your inner child within. (Put dab of oil on the forehead in a spiral mark).

"You are a precious child of the Light. Receive God's blessing for your life."

Leader - Light Bearers and Children of the Light, go forth now to carry the teachings of all the Messengers of Light in your hearts and to share the peace, love, hope and joy that is ours. May the Holy Ones bless you and keep you now and forever more.

CEREMONY OF REMEMBRANCE
(A Memorial Day ceremony for those who have passed on into the Light)

People have been celebrating life and death during the change from harvest to winter for over 10,000 years. Many religious traditions have grown out of the knowledge that the veils between the physical and spiritual worlds are very thin at this change of the season.

Many people choose to make their transitions at this time of peace. Within that peace there is an awareness of the presence of Angels. Many people making their transition see the Angels in their rooms, standing quietly behind their loved ones. They often talk to the Angels and Loved Ones who have gone before them.

Some cultures believe their Loved Ones are not gone from their lives, but simply have taken on a new form. The family still talks to them and receives guidance. It is important for all of us to remember our family members and friends who have gone before us. This ceremony is to help us remember their lives and all they taught us.

Supplies: Pictures to display of Loved Ones to remember; a candle and lighter.

Instructions: Each person is invited to bring a picture of a deceased love one to share. The candle is lighted to begin the ceremony.

Opening

Leader: We are gathered to honor the memory of our Loved Ones who have gone before us. Their presence is still felt in our lives and their teachings continue to guide us. We know that each of our Loved Ones is now in the Presence of the Angels and the Divine Spirit that created us all. One day we will join them in the Light. It is important for us to remember them for their legacy lives on in us.

Let us pray: *Divine Mother-Father-God, we give thanks for your messengers, the Angels, and the heavenly work they do to protect and uplift us at those precious moments when we need to feel your presence. We ask that the Angels be with us now as we remember our beloved family and friends who have passed on to the Light. We pray for their continued growth and evolvement on the other side, in that great Paradise of Eternal Love. We know you keep them safe in your Loving Arms and that one day we too will join them in that holy and sacred place we call Heaven. And, so it is.*

Song

Please join me now in singing "Amazing Grace" (or other appropriate song.)

Sharing

Leader: I invite you now to show the pictures of your Loved Ones, tell us a little something about them and share a memory or a teaching that has helped you in your life. After each sharing we will say together:

"At the rising of the sun and the rising of the moon, we will remember you."

Prayer for Transformation.

Let us pray. *Heavenly Father-Mother-God, Great Spirit of Life and Rebirth, we know that You have taken our loved ones in Your Loving Hands and given them peace. We know that You have transformed them from the limitations of the physical world into the wondrous beings of Light that is their true form. Make them shine like the sun with Your Radiance. Help them leave the trials and challenges of this world behind them and claim the beauty and serenity of the spiritual world. If any of our loved ones are lost in the between time, reach out Your Hand to them and lead them Home. We pray for ourselves that we may remember and know that death is only a doorway into that glorious world to which we all belong. And that our loved ones will be there to greet us and welcome us Home. In the Name Which We Hold Most Holy, we pray. And, so it is.*

Leader: Let us honor our Loved Ones by doing a special act of kindness for someone else in the name of our Loved Ones during this coming week.

Go now in peace and may your Loved Ones be remembered for the Light they brought to your life and to this world.

CEREMONY OF REMEMBRANCE FOR VETERANS DAY

The men and women who have served or are now serving in the military deserve to be remembered and blessed. They hold a special place of honor in society. Their job is to protect and defend us. They are our heroes and heroines. Even if we support peace, we must honor our military heroes and heroines, for their real purpose is to protect our peace and to bring peace to the world.

This ceremony can be held at home, with friends, in a park, or in a cemetery. It is a solemn occasion and is done with gratitude and appreciation.

Supplies: Pictures of our military heroes and heroines, deceased or still living; small American flags to place on graves or in home-gardens; flowers and/or candles. Chairs for the honored veterans.

Instructions: If the ceremony is done at home or indoors, the pictures can be placed on a small table. If the ceremony is done outdoors, the pictures may be held by the family. After the opening there is a time for sharing. The flags are placed in an appropriate place to close the ceremony.

Opening

Leader: This is a day to remember the American men and women who gave their lives for what they believed in and a day to remember all those who are serving in the military today. It is also a day to remember all the veterans from all the wars all over the world, who believed they were fighting for right and justice.

When the Civil War was over, the women of both sides came together to plant flowers on all the graves, North and South alike, to honor all the men who fought for peace. From this simple act of compassion, Veterans Day was born. We follow their example today and honor the veterans from all the wars.

Will all veterans and military personnel please stand? Your community is so grateful for your service and each of us offers our sincere appreciation for all that you have done. (If the veterans are a small group, they are invited to say their name, rank, and branch of service.) You may be seated.

Let us join together in silent meditation for a few moments, breathing deeply and bringing peace to this gathering of remembrance.

I am a lamp to you that behold me. I am a mirror to you that perceive me. I am a door to you that knock upon me. I am a way to you the traveler. --The Bible

Music Solo or Group Song (God Bless America)

Sharing

Leader: I invite you now to come forward and remember your veteran or military service person by saying their names and their branch of service. We will repeat the litany "At the rising of the sun and rising of the moon, we will remember you" after each name. It is important that we remember our loved ones, for their legacy lives on in us. We are one Family, One Spirit, One Life. (Names are shared.)

Prayer for Transformation

Let us pray. *Heavenly Father-Mother-God, Great Spirit of Life and Rebirth, we know that You have taken our loved ones in Your Loving Arms and have given them peace. We know that You have transformed them from the limitations of the physical world into the wondrous beings of Light that is their true form. Make them shine like the sun with Your Radiance. Help them leave the trials and challenges of this world behind them and claim the beauty and serenity of the spiritual world. If any of our loved ones are lost in the between time, reach out Your Hand to them and lead them Home.*

We pray for our veterans who are still among us. Lighten their burdens and heal the wounds of war. Help them to recognize the gifts they have given to us and continue to brighten their lives. Bless them with love and peace. We pray for all the men and women who have fought and died for their beliefs no matter what country they were born in. Hold them all in Your Loving Arms and comfort them and bring to them the peace for which they fought, for we are One People united through the love of the Divine Spirit, though we call You by many names. We pray for peace in the world today and for all the generations to come. In the Name Which We Hold Most Holy. And, so it is.

Closing Song

Let us sing together "Amazing Grace" (or a similar closing song).

Closing Blessing

May the peace of God be with you now and forever more.

Participants may come forward and shake the hands of the veterans with gratitude and appreciation for their service.

Cultural and Religious Ceremonies

Catharine Gates

CULTURAL AND RELIGIOUS CEREMONIES

❀

There is beauty in our diversity, our beliefs, and our traditions. These ceremonies honor our diversity. They are not orthodox ceremonies but contain the essential spirit of the traditional and universal religious meanings. We honor each culture, each people, each religion by participating in the ceremonies with reverence and respect.

You are encouraged to honor your own culture and religion by adding important ceremonies and celebrations into the life of your family. These memories of coming together in a sacred way are cherished by the children and the grandparents alike. They bind us together as family and as a culture. They remind us that with our diversity, we are one people, one humanity.

SEDER CEREMONY - JEWISH

The Seder Ceremony and Dinner has been held continuously by the Jewish people for over 3000 years. It is held during Passover in the spring. It celebrates the journey of the Children of Israel out of slavery in the land of Egypt to freedom in the Promised Land. It is also the story of today as we celebrate the struggle for our freedom. Since this is a modern ceremony, it may also include non-Jewish people. The prayers are traditional Seder prayers. (*Yamakas* (ceremonial hats) *for men and head coverings for women* are optional.)

Supplies: Special menu (see Appendix); bottles of wine or sparkling juice, enough for each participant to have 4 small glasses; an empty cup for Elijah; 3 tapers for the Seder Candles; washing bowls, pitchers and paper towels; matzah crackers, bitter herbs (parsley sprigs), and small bowls of salty water for dipping. One symbolic Seder Plate with a bone (lamb or symbol of bone), parsley or romaine lettuce, apple salad, and matzah crackers. This is used as part of the ceremony. Copies of the ceremony so guest can follow along and recite the prayers.

Instructions: This is an interactive ceremony and has a special order with special prayers to say at the proper times. Appoint one or two people from each table to pour the juice and carry the hand washing supplies. Place small dishes of parsley and small bowls of salty water on each table. Set an empty place and empty cup for the prophet Elijah. Guests are seated as the ceremony begins.

Opening

Leader: Welcome to our Seder ceremony and dinner. The official Passover for the Jewish people begins at sundown this year on _____ and lasts for a week. The date changes every year. Passover has been celebrated for over 3,000 years during the spring celebration of Pesach. It celebrates the journey of the Children of Israel out of slavery in Egypt to freedom in the Promised Land. It celebrates the miracles of God. It is not only the story of the Children of Israel, but it is also our own story. We are asked during this Seder ceremony to imagine what it is like to be a slave, like the Children of Israel, and what freedom meant to them and to us. We celebrate freedom and remember all the people in the world who are not yet free. May this Seder light a torch of freedom for all people of the world. We begin by lighting the Seder Candles.

Lighting the Seder Candles

Let us be in an attitude of prayer as _____lights our Seder Candles. (Wise Woman wearing a shawl over her hair lights candles and moves her hands over the flames three times in a reverent manner saying a silent prayer.)

Service

Leader: Please follow along with the service printed in your booklet. Join me in saying the first prayer together:

> *Blessed art thou, Lord, our God, Master of the Universe, who sanctifies us with your commandments, and commands us to kindle the light of this Passover. Blessed art thou, Lord, our God, who has kept us alive and sustained us, and has brought us to this special time.*

Kiddush - First Cup of Wine

During this Seder we will drink four cups of wine (we use sparkling juice). Wine is a symbol of joy, happiness, and transformation. We drink four cups in remembrance of the four corners of the universe for we seek freedom everywhere. They also represent the four seasons for freedom must be guarded at all times.

The cups represent the four promises made by God – "I will bring you out – I will deliver you – I will redeem you – I will take you to be my people." This first cup of wine stands for physical freedom, being able to move around as we choose. Let us say the blessing together and drink the first cup of wine. (Volunteers pour first cup of juice)

> *Blessed are you, Lord our God, Ruler of the Universe, Creator of the fruit of the vine.*

Urchatz – Purification – Washing of the Hands

We wash our hands to purify them and as a sign of respect. (Volunteers take around the pitchers, washing bowls, and paper towels.)

Karpas – Green Vegetable

Pesach is a spring holiday reminding us that life is renewed every year. Karpas, the green vegetable (parsley), reminds us of springtime and hope. We dip the karpas in salty water to remind us of tears. We remember the tears of our people when they suffered in Egypt and our own tears when we suffer. May we never be so complacent that we forget or ignore the tears of others who are suffering. Let us dip the karpas in the salty water, say the blessing together and eat it.

Blessed are you, Lord our God, Ruler of the Universe, Creator of the fruit of the earth.

Yachatz – Breaking the Matzah

When the Children of Israel fled out of Egypt, they did not have time to let their bread rise so they baked unleavened bread to take on their journey. We break the Matzah on the Seder Plate in three pieces representing the 3 symbols of life – God, the Torah (the Book of the Laws) and Israel, (the soul, the mind and the heart.) We break the matzah in remembrance of the miracle of God that split the Red Sea, so the people could walk on dry land. Broken matzah also symbolizes the broken matzah of speech and that words are to be used for healing and making whole rather than broken and used to hurt. We invite all who are hungry to join us and pray that all people everywhere will be free. (Break the middle piece of matzah and return the smaller piece to the plates.)

Maggid – the Haggadah – The Four Questions –and the Story of the Exodus

During the Seder dinner it is customary for the children to ask the Four Questions. Children are encouraged to ask questions of their Elders, to seek answers for themselves. (Ask a child to read the questions.)

Why is this night different from all other nights?

Why only matzah?

Why the dipping?

Why do we eat the bitter herbs?

(1) This night is different from all other nights because we remember our ancestors and the courage it took to pack up everything they owned and take their families to freedom. (2) We eat the matzah, the unleavened bread in remembrance of the three symbols of life-which no one can take away from us. (3) We dip the karpas into the salty water to remind us of the tears of our people when they suffered in Egypt and our own tears when we suffer. (4) We eat the bitter herbs to remind us not to be complacent or forget that others are still suffering and in bondage.

We tell the story again, so we can remember and to teach our children about freedom.

3,000 years ago, the Children of Israel were held captive in Egypt. This is the story of people everywhere who come out of slavery into freedom. The Hebrew people came to Egypt in the time of Joseph who rose to great heights in Egypt and helped take care of the people during the great famine. After many years, the new Pharaoh became afraid that the Hebrew people would not obey him and made them slaves. They had to make bricks and build great cities and had little to eat. Moses was born at this time and his mother put him into a small basket on the river, so he would not become a slave. Pharaoh's daughter found him and took him for her own son. Moses grew up in the Palace as a royal Egyptian prince. When he was a man, he learned he was not an Egyptian, but a Hebrew. God commanded him to lead the people out of slavery to the Promised Land. Pharaoh did not want to let the people go, so God sent ten plagues to the land of Egypt, and finally Pharaoh was forced to let the people leave. When we recall the plagues, we take a drop of wine from our glass in remembrance of the sufferings of the Egyptians. Pharaoh changed his mind and sent his army after the people, but God parted the Sea of Reeds, so they could pass safely over the land. When the Sea returned, the Egyptian army was trapped and drowned. From the Reed Sea, the people wandered for forty years in the desert and finally came to Mount Sinai where God gave Moses the Torah, the Books of the Law, and the Ten Commandments. From there the people finally reached the Promised Land.

Midrash – Washing the Hands

We wash our hands again in preparation for the feast.

Second Cup of Wine

This time we only pour half a cup to remember that even in our gladness we must remember the sufferings of others. This second cup of wine symbolizes the freedom of the mind. We open our minds to new ideas and try to understand the ideas and beliefs of others. Knowledge and understanding will lead to a world of freedom. Let us say the blessing together. And then drink the second cup of wine.

*Blessed are you, Lord our God, Ruler of the Universe, Creator of the fruit of the Vine.

Pesach, Matzah and Maror

The Seder Plate holds the symbols for the story. The Pesach or bone symbolizes the lamb, which was worshipped by the Egyptians. It represents the rejection of idolatry. When we put ourselves or others in the place of God, we limit our spiritual freedom.

The Matzah represents the unleavened bread. We eat the matzah to remind us to be vigilant and respect our freedom.

The Maror, the bitter herb, (parsley or romaine lettuce) represents the bitterness of slavery and the bitterness of our tears when we are enslaved to any others, or to any false thought or feeling.

The apple salad we will eat later represents the mortar put between the bricks. Our faith is the mortar that holds the foundations of our lives together.

(Take up the three pieces of the Matzah with the broken one in between like a sandwich. Then, let the bottom Matzah drop back onto the plate and recite the blessing together and then eat the Matzah. Then dip the maror (romaine lettuce) into the salt water and eat it.) Let us say the blessing together.

Blessed are you, Lord our God, who makes us holy with commandments and commands us to eat matzah, maror and pesach.

Shulchan Orech – the Feast

We remember together what it felt like to be a slave in Egypt, how wonderful it feels to be free, and how God takes care of us and leads us to our rightful place. Now we enjoy the feast of our freedom. Hardboiled eggs are a part of the Seder Feast and represent the Jewish people, as a Rabbi explained, "The more an egg is burned or boiled, the harder it gets." Let us enjoy our meal. (Note: We serve the meal buffet style)

Tzafun – Out of Hiding - Eating the Afikoman

Now for our dessert, we eat the large piece of Matzah that we broke off at the beginning of the meal. It represents the sacrifice that is always eaten last. (Pass around last piece of Matzah and everyone takes a bite to eat.)

The Third Cup of Wine

The Third Cup of Wine symbolizes spiritual freedom. Let us seek the spiritual freedom that generations before us sacrificed to maintain. Let us open our hearts and minds to experience God in our own lives. Let us say together the blessing.

Blessed are you, Lord our God, Ruler of the Universe, Creator of the fruit of the vine.

Barech – Blessing After the Meal

Grace is always said after the meal in Jewish tradition. Let us say this grace together.

Let us praise God. Praised be the name of God for ever and ever! Blessed is our God of whose abundance we have eaten and by whose goodness we live. The Lord will give strength to His people and God will bless us with peace. Amien.

The Fourth Cup of Wine - Elijah's Cup

Our fourth and final cup of wine is filled. We also fill a cup for Elijah, the Prophet, the harbinger of the coming Messiah. We open the door to invite Elijah in. (Ask a child to open the door to see if

Elijah is waiting to enter). Elijah's cup represents messianic freedom, the promise of a deeper spiritual understanding. We cannot drink out of Elijah's cup until the world is whole and at peace, until justice and compassion reign. We welcome you, Spirit of Elijah, into our homes and into our hearts. May your message inspire us to become God's partners in bringing about peace. Let us recite the blessing for Elijah and drink our final cup of wine

> *Elijah the Prophet, Elijah the Tishbite, Elijah the Gileadite, may he soon come and bring the Messiah, the son of David.*

Song of Praise

The Seder service ends with a song of praise to God, the Lord of the entire universe, known by many names. Let us stand and sing together. (A CD of a Jewish song may be played or other appropriate song.)

Nirtzah – Acceptance

And now we greet each other and say with heartfelt gratitude and anticipation of the coming world of peace and freedom that the City of Jerusalem represents: "Next year in Jerusalem!" (Guests greet each other with this phrase and the celebration ends.)

Note: A sample menu for a modern Seder dinner is in the Appendix. We serve the meal buffet style.

HO'OPONOPONO CEREMONY OF FORGIVENESS – HAWAIIAN

This ceremony is based on the Hawaiian concept of *pono – making right*. It refers to the power of forgiveness. Forgiveness is the basis of all healing, especially the forgiveness of the self for incorrect perception. It can be done indoors or in an outdoor setting. (One of the most beautiful ceremonies we did was in British Columbia at a workshop beside a beautiful lake with a smooth beach. Washing our hands in the waters of the lake at the end of the ceremony was very moving.)

This ceremony is based on the work of Dr. Haleaka Hew Len and Mornah Nalamaku Simeona. (For more information, check out ho'oponopono online). Hawaiian music, especially chants, enhance the experience of this ceremony.

We decorate the altar table with Hawaiian cloths, shells and bead leis. We also provide leis for all participants to wear. After the ceremony we have a luau feast featuring Hawaiian food or any dish made with pineapple. Fresh fruit is always a welcome addition to the feast.

Supplies: A small bowl of anointing oil or olive oil; pitcher of scented water (cinnamon is good), bowl, paper towels, small trash container. Booklets of the Order of the Ceremony with the Prayers. A volunteer to help with the washing of the hands.

Instructions: Set up an altar table with Hawaiian items. Place the pitcher of warm scented water and the towels, already separated, on one end of the table with the trash container nearby and the anointing oil on the other end. During the ceremony people will wash their hands at one end and move to the other end for the anointing.

Opening

Leader: Aloha and welcome to this special ceremony of forgiveness. This is a solemn ceremony and you are invited to participate in a reverent manner. During the ceremony, we will be taking the Ha La, the Breath of Light, which is four deep breaths visualizing the Light of the Divine filling our lungs on the inbreath and breathing out forgiveness on the outbreath. We will also be washing our hands symbolizing that we have cleansed away all hurts. We will then be anointed with the holy oil as a sign that we have been forgiven. I ask that you participate in this ceremony of forgiveness whole heartedly as all healing begins with forgiveness. We will say the Responses together.

Music
Hawaiian Chants

Inspirational Reading

Leader: Hear this wisdom from the Ancient Hawaiians:

"Know that there is a path to a higher consciousness within ourselves…and you alone are keeper of that path…a path that can be blocked by the events of life." Make amends for the wrong you have done to others and rid yourselves of guilt. Free yourselves from feelings of injustice…and injustice will no longer stalk you. Your suffering is only caused by your thoughts. You are in charge of your mind…free it. No difficulty has any power over you unless you give it that power. Let past events fade away and don't allow them to paint dark colors on your future." –Kristin Zambucka in "Ano Ano, the Seed."

I invite you to be in an attitude of humbleness, sincerity, and awareness as we sit in the silence for a few minutes preparing for this ceremony of forgiveness.

Opening Prayer

Let us pray; *Beloved Aumakua, we come before you in this ho'oponopono gathering and ask the Aumakuas, the Higher Selves, of each and every person here, to gather with us as the Poe Aumakua, the Great Gathering of the Higher Selves. We open our hearts to change by forgiving those who have hurt us and by forgiving ourselves for hurting others. We ask that you be with us now and that if any person cannot receive our sincere atonement, bring them into the Light and let your Love balance and bring peace to their souls. In your Holy Name we pray. And, so it is.*

Breath of Light – Ha La (Leader slowly counts breaths, 1,2,3,4)

Let us take four breaths, breathing in the Light of Forgiveness from the Divine and breathing out forgiveness to yourself, your family, your community and to the world. As you breathe, ask your inner self to hold the energy until requested to release it.

Blessing of the Water and the Oil

Great Gathering of our Higher Selves, we ask your blessings on this water that it might be transformed into Holy Water, to cleanse, purify and release us, offender and offended. Let it cleanse away forever all of the unwanted and negative memories that have blocked our path to you.

Great Gathering of our Higher Selves, we ask your blessings on this oil that it might be transformed into Holy Oil, that will mark us as forgiven in your grace. And, so it is.

Leader: Raise your arms and release this energy to the Higher Selves to bless this water and oil.

Breath of Light –Ha La

Prayer of Self-Forgiveness

Leader: From the awareness of the mind-self we say this prayer to the heart-self:

My dearest Little Sister or Brother, I unconditionally and sincerely forgive you now for any and all hurts, whatever they have been, whenever they occurred. I truly love you.

Response: I forgive you now.

Will you forgive me for not listening, for not acting on your instincts and communications, for shutting you out, for not showing how much I really care about you, and for all the other hurts I have caused you? PLEASE FORGIVE ME NOW.

Response: Yes, I forgive you.

Leader: Release the energy and direct it to your inner self by placing your hands on your heart.

Breath of Light -Ha La

Forgiveness of Others

Call to mind now any person or persons in your life whom you see as having hurt you and affirm your desire to forgive them. Silently in your heart sincerely forgive them. If a person is no longer in a physical body or not available, send the forgiveness to your Higher Self. Release all hurts, feelings of being offended, and all unkind thoughts. Affirm you will no longer cling to the old hurts. If you feel any residue of the old hurts in any part of your body, pull them out and give them to your Higher Self to be transformed back into Light. Do this for each person you wish to forgive. (Allow time for this process.)

Call to mind now any person or persons you have hurt and affirm your desire to ask for and be forgiven. Make a promise to yourself that you will go to that person and ask for forgiveness for any and all hurts and offenses you have caused. If that person is no longer in a physical body or not available, send the request to your Higher Self and ask to be forgiven. Do this for each and every person you have harmed in any way. (Allow time for this process.)

Response. You are now forgiven.

Leader: Release the energy to your Higher Self.

Breath of Light -Ha La

Prayer for Forgiveness for the Family

Divine Spirit, if we, our families, relatives and ancestors have offended any individual, family, relative or ancestor in thoughts, words, or actions, from the beginning of our creation to the present, HUMBLY, HUMBLY, HUMBLY we ask you to forgive all our errors, resentments, unkind thoughts, and words or deeds, which we have created and accumulated from the beginning to the present. PLEASE FORGIVE US! PLEASE FORGIVE US! PLEASE FORGIVE US!

Response: You are forgiven!

Leader: Release the energy to your Higher Self.

The Ritual of Cleansing

We invite you now to come forward to ritually cleanse yourself of all obstructions or blocks by washing your hands in the Holy Water and receiving the mark of forgiveness with the Holy Oil. (Volunteer helps with hand washing and Leader does the anointing.)

Leader (anointing the forehead of each participant): *"Child of Light, receive this sign that you are forgiven and loved so very much."*

Breath of Light - Ha La

Affirmation of Forgiveness (Everyone)

I am now ready and willing to receive the perfecting presence of my Higher Self in my life. I am now thankful for the mercy, joy and love that this life has bestowed upon me. I have now forgiven myself for every thought, word and deed I have embraced or undertaken that has kept me from the realization of the Truth about myself and the perfect unfolding of the Divine Plan for my life.

I have now forgiven everyone for every thought, word, and deed they have embraced or undertaken that has kept them from the realization of the Truth about themselves and me, and the perfect unfolding of the Divine Plan for our lives. I have forgiven all! I release all! I am now free from all, except the perfect and Divine Plan and purpose for my life!

For this I am so very grateful! And so it is!

Leader: Release the energy to your Higher Self.

Breath of Light – Ha La

Closing Prayer of Healing

Leader: *Beloved Higher Selves, we thank you for this healing of forgiveness. Let Divine Order, Light, Love, Peace, Balance, Understanding, Joy, Abundance and Wisdom be manifest for us now. We are whole and perfect. May your spirit proceed us in every word, thought and deed from this moment forward as we live the hurtless and loving life in service to humanity. In your name and in the names of the Great Gathering of Higher Selves, we know that it is done. And so it is!*

Leader: Release the energy to your Higher Self with gratitude.

Amama ua noa. Lele wale Akua La. Our prayer has taken flight. Let the rain of blessings fall.

KWANZAA – AFRICAN AMERICAN

Kwanzaa (**Kwahn**-zah) is a new ritual of celebration, designed in 1966 by Dr. Maulana Karengo, to help people of color remember their heritage and to build pride in the principles of community that have come to us from Africa. The spiritual traditions of the African people are rich and profound. They are based on community rather than individuals and form the foundation for working and growing together as one people, one heart and one mind. Kwanzaa, is a Swahili word which means "first fruits," and it is based on Kawaida, the African communitarian philosophy which teaches that values are "the hinge on which human possibilities turn." Many of the rituals and symbols come from other African cultures. It has grown to be celebrated internationally.

Beginning on December 26th, Kwanzaa is celebrated for seven days. Each evening the family gathers together to light the candle that represents the principle for that day and to discuss what that means on a personal level and a family and community level. They also talk about how they will practice that principle for the next year. The last day, January 1st, is spent in meditation and quiet reflecting on these questions:

Who am I?

Am I Really Who I Say I Am?

Am I All I Ought to Be?

There are seven symbols for Kwanzaa. The woven **mat** which represents the foundation of the community, all the other symbols are placed on the mat. An ear of **corn** is placed on the mat for each child in the family. If there are no children, one ear represents the potential for children. The **fruits** and nuts represent the rewards of collective and productive labor. The **Kinara** or the Kwanzaa candleholder. (Seven **candles** represent the seven principles of Kwanzaa: three red candles represent the struggle of the African peoples; three green candles represent the fruitful future; one black candle represents the African people. The red and green candles are lit alternately, one each day, to show that without struggle there is no future).

The Unity **cup** represents unity as the foundation of life. It also represents the unity of the past, the present and the future, and honors the ancestors and their struggles for us. Handmade heritage **gifts** are given by the parents to the children during Kwanzaa and represent the rich culture of Africa. The final symbol is the flag of red, green and black.

Supplies:– Woven mat on which are placed the other symbols; ear of corn for each child in the family; fruits and nuts, Kinara, candle holder for 7 candles; unity cup; handmade heritage gifts; and the flag of red, green and black. Elder volunteer to drink the libation.

Instructions: Practice **Harambee** (ha-ram-**bay**-ay) by raising the right arm with an open hand and as you bring it down, you make it into a fist and say Harambee. This is done seven times throughout the ceremony.

Practice the **Kwanzaa Dance:** Take 4 small steps in place with your hands at shoulder height and your pointer fingers pointing upward. Then do three wing moves with your arms and on the fourth count hug yourself. The final four counts are done by putting your weight on your heels and extending your hands in front of you with palms up and rotating them in a circle toward the center.

Opening

Leader: The spiritual traditions of the African people are rich and profound. They are based on community rather than individuals and form the foundation for working and growing together as one people, one heart and one mind. It is through community that we learn how to live together in peace. It is through community that we learn we can make a difference. It is through community that we become mindful caretakers of our Mother Earth. Kwanzaa is a year-end celebration meant for all people of the world, to draw them back to their roots and the spiritual principles that bind us all together.

Let us pray: *Heavenly Creator of All the Universe, we give thanks this day for this opportunity to come together as a community, to light the Candles of Kwanzaa, to honor our ancestors, and to think and talk about the important values that bind us together as one people. And, so it is.*

Let us practice the Harambee which we will do after each section.

Harambee (ha-ram-**bay**-ay) is done by raising the right arm with an open hand and as you bring it down, you make it into a fist and say Harambee. This is repeated seven times.

Song

Let us sing "Kumbayah" which is Gullah for "Come by here."

The Tambiko (Tam-bee-koh):

Our fathers and mothers came here, lived, loved, struggled and built here. At this place their love and labor rose like the sun and gave strength and meaning to the day. For them, then, who gave so much we give in return. On this same soil we will sow our seeds and build and move in unity and strength. Here we too we continue their struggle for liberation and a higher level of human life. May our eyes be the eagle, our strength be the elephant, and the boldness of our life be like the lion. And may we remember and honor our ancestors and the legacy they left for as long as the sun shines and the waters flow. We ask _____, one of our honored Elders, to come forward to pour the libation and to take a drink for all of us. (Pour the libation and drink.)

Let us take a few moments to reflect on one of the Elders in our own families who influenced our lives in a positive way and then we will go around the room and say their names out loud to honor them. **Harambee.**

Lighting of the Mshumaa: (Em-shoo-ma-ah)

Every evening during Kwanzaa, one candle is lighted. (They may all be lit if there is only ceremony.) The Kwanzaa candles are lighted by a young person. Will _____ come forward to help us light the Kwanzaa candles?

As we light each candle, I will ask the question, Habare Ganah (Ha-**bah**-ree **Gah**-nah) What's new? Everyone answers with the next of the Nguzo Saba, (n-**goo**-zoh **saw**-baw) the Seven Principles. (Light candles and ask Habare Ganah?)

Umoja (Unity) To strive for and maintain unity in the family, community, nation and race.

Kujichagulia (Self-Determination) To define ourselves, name ourselves, create for ourselves and speak for ourselves.

Ujima (Collective Work and Responsibility) To build and maintain our community together and make our brother's and sister's problems our problems and to solve them together.

Ujamaa (Cooperative Economics) To build and maintain our own stores, shops, and other businesses and to profit from them

Nia (Purpose) To make our collective vocation the building and developing of our community in order to restore our people to their traditional greatness.

Kuumba (Creativity) To do always as much as we can, in the way we can, in order to leave our community more beautiful and beneficial than we inherited it.

Imani (Faith) To believe with all our heart in our people, our parents, our teachers, our leaders and the righteousness and victory of our struggle.

Harambee.

Passing of the Gifts, the Fruits and Nuts

The dried fruits and nuts are passed out to everyone who takes and eats some.

Kwanzaa Dance

Diections: Take 4 small steps in place with your hands at shoulder height and your pointer fingers pointing upward. Then do three wing moves with your arms and the final count hug yourself. The final four counts are done by putting your weight on your heels and extending your hands in front of you with palms up and rotating them in a circle toward the center.

Closing Prayer

Please join hands for our closing prayer: Let us pray: *Heavenly Creator of All the Universe, we give thanks this day for this opportunity to come together as a community, to light the Candles of Kwanzaa, to honor our ancestors, and to think and talk about the important values that bind us together as one people. May we remember who we really are and to be that person in every moment. Help us to be all that we truly are and to make a difference in our families, our community, and in the world. And, so it is.*

WICCA – BELTANE PLANTING RITUAL

Beltane is a time to joyously celebrate the return of the sun, the flowering of trees and the planting of seeds for food and happiness for the earth-based religious. This ritual is typically done on the eve of Beltane, which is April 30th. We celebrate this change of seasons with a Planting Ritual, part of which is done during the ceremony and part of which is done at home.

Supplies: Bowl of soil on a tray with a spoon; bowl of pea seeds; pot or paper cup and a slip of paper and pencil for each participant; 1-2 assistants to pass around the soil, the seeds and the pitcher of water.

Instructions: The oldest person in the family should lead the ritual. Give each participant a cup and a slip of paper and pencil as they enter the circle. Participants write their names on their cups.

Leader: We are planting seeds and planting our prayers for abundance and happiness.

Welcome, spring!
The light has returned, and life has come back to the earth
The soil is dark and full of energy
so this day we plant our seeds
They will lie in the soil, taking root and growing
until the time has come for them to meet the sun.
As we plant these seeds, we give thanks to the earth
for its strength and life-bringing gifts.

The Planting

Leader: Now is the time for preparing for our seeds. Fill your cup halfway with the soil. (An assistant passes around the tray with the bowl of soil with a spoon to fill the cups.) We will sing this song as the cups are filled. (Or another suitable song).

Round and round the Earth is turning,
Turning always round 'til morning
And from morning round to night.

Leader: Now we plant our seeds. Please take four seeds, the symbol for the four seasons, and push them into the soil in your cup. (Another assistant passes around the bowl of seeds) We will sing our song again as the seeds are planted.)

Round and round the Earth is turning,
Turning always round 'til morning
And from morning round to night.

Leader: Tiny seeds, containing life! They travel upon the wind and bring to us abundance. Flowers, herbs, vegetables, fruit, all the bounty of the earth. *We give thanks to the seeds and for the gifts that are to come in the harvest season.*

Seeds need water to grow so now we will pour a small amount of water on our seeds. Come forward to the altar table, pour a little water to dampen your seeds, and place your cup on the altar table to be blessed and return to your seat.

Water, cool and life-giving brings power to these seeds and moisture to this fertile soil. We give thanks to the water for allowing life to bloom once more.

Take out your piece of paper and pencil or pen and write down on your paper something that you wish to see bloom in your life. (Harmony, happiness, financial security, strong relationships, healing, etc.). Hold your paper in your hand and bless it.

Today, we plant seeds in the earth, but Beltane is a time in which many things can grow. Today, we plant seeds in our hearts and souls, for other things we wish to see blossom. We plant the seeds of love, of wisdom, of happiness. We dig deep, and begin a crop of harmony, balance, and joy. We add water to bring life and abundance of all kinds into our homes. We offer our prayers for the seedlings as they carry our wishes from Mother Earth out to the Universe.

Now fold up the paper and put it somewhere safe and when you take your planted seeds home, dig a hole out in the yard, or in a pot, or you can leave your seeds in the cup until they sprout, and then plant them. Place the piece of paper with your wish in the bottom of the hole. Carefully remove the soil and seeds from your cup and place them in the hole. Make sure the seeds are pressed gently down into the soil. Gently water your seeds and remember to water them every day. Say your own prayer as you plant your seeds. The seeds will send down roots into your wish and then down into Mother Earth. When they sprout, they will send your prayers upward to Spirit. The plants symbolize the wish you want to see blooming in your life so take good care of your seeds and sprouts and know that your wish is being fulfilled.

Let us offer a prayer for these seeds and wishes for Beltane:

O God who reveals your Spirit through the Goddess at this time of year, we ask that these seeds be blessed. We ask that the planters be blessed with the manifestation of his or her wishes that these seeds represent. May we all grow into beauty fulfilling the sacred gifts you have given us. Thank you for the blessings of spring, for the richness of the blessings of the Goddess, and for all the blessings of our lives. So, mote it be!

Closing Circle

Form a Circle and end the Ceremony with a closing song.

LUGHNASA/LAMMAS RITUAL

Lughnasa (Lu-**na**-sa), the ancient Celtic celebration of Lugh, the Sun-King, the God of Light and Life is celebrated between August 1 and September 1. Fire is an important symbol of this celebration and the festivals always centered around great bonfires. Lugh is personified as the God of Life at this time of year as the crops, which must be cut down for the survival of the people. This festival honors his great sacrifice and the first Harvest of the Year as the crops are reaped.

The early Saxons celebrated this time as Lammas or Loaf Mass. In this festival the Corn King is sacrificed so the people can live. He moves through the darkness of his death into the womb of the Great Mother, so he can be reborn again in Midwinter as the Child of Light at the Winter Solstice.

Both of these festivals are about death and rebirth, about the great cycle of Life. The grain is ceremonially harvested, reaped, ground into flour, and baked into bread, usually in the form of a man. Eating this first bread of the Harvest, the bread of the Gods, gives us life.

Supplies and Setup: Chair set up in a circle; a loaf of bread, homemade and baked into the shape of a person; apple juice or cider and cups; pitcher of warm water and a bowl; paper towels. (Volunteers to carry the water, the bread and the juice.)

Instructions: This ritual is similar to the communion ritual of the Christian church. There is some discussion that the ritual of communion is developed from this pagan ceremony.

Opening

Leader: Take a deep breath and bring yourself into your sacred space as we pray this ancient prayer.

Now is the time of the First Harvest when the bounties of nature give of themselves so that we may survive. O God of the ripening fields, Lord of the Grain, Grant us the understanding of sacrifice as you prepare to deliver yourself under the sickle of the Goddess and journey to the lands of eternal summer. O Goddess of the dark moon, teach us the secrets of rebirth, as the Sun loses its strength and nights grow cold. Teach us of patience, of nurturing, and hope. In the Holy Names of That Which We Hold Sacred. So, mote it be!

Cleansing

We first cleanse our hands as a symbol that we are free from all grudges and revengeful thoughts and ready to be blessed. (Pass around the pitcher of water and bowl Each participant washes the hands.)

Partaking and Sharing of the Bread

Reverently take a piece of this harvest loaf of bread symbolizing the fruits of the first harvest of the year, knowing it is given for you. Break off a small bite, enough to feed two people. First offer the bite to your neighbor on your right saying, "Eat of the Bread of Life. May you never go hungry." The neighbor eats the bread. You eat the last bite saying to yourself, "As we eat this Bread of Life, may we remember to feed those who have no bread." (Pass the bread)

Take a cup of this juice from the tray and pass it to the neighbor on your left, saying, "May you never go thirsty." (Pass the juice and all drink)

Closing Prayer

Let us pray. *Creator of All Life, thank you for all that has been raised from the soil. We thank you for the fruits of the harvest and for the never-ending fruits of your love. Let your strength and power grow in us as the strength and power of your love grows in all our relationships. We thank you for the promise of fruits to come. So, mote it be!*

Special Ceremonies

SPECIAL CEREMONIES

———— ❁ ————

These special ceremonies are blessings for homes, businesses, and those spaces in which traumatic events have taken place. The final ceremony is a model for ceremonies held around a Peace Pole.

HOME CLEANSING, BLESSING, AND DEDICATION

Homes are our greater bodies, the space we create around us. Our home should be quiet, and serene, a haven of retreat. Blessings for homes should be done every year, when a person moves to a different home, or when a new home is ready to be occupied. This ritual is done in two parts. First the home is cleansed, cleared of all negative energies. Then the home is blessed and a symbol of what the family wants to create in the new home is blessed and buried or placed in a box near the front door.

Supplies: Altar cloth, salt, water, oil for blessing, incense or sage, 2 candles, some object representing the family from the old house, a glass of water, bread and cheese and an apple; symbols of what the family wants to create in the new home; drums and rattles.

Instructions: Set up the altar in the center of the home or in the kitchen which represents the modern hearth or heart of the home. On a special cloth, set out the 2 candles, the sage, water, salt, oil and symbol from the old house. Also include a symbol for the new house.

The Gathering

The householder will light the first candle on the altar. *"We bring to light this guardian flame, to cast all shadows back from whence they came."* Envision a Great Circle of Golden Light encompassing the hearth, the house and the property

Leader: We are gathered here to bless this house.

We call upon the Creators of All Life, The Great Spirit, the Keepers of the Four Directions, the Ancestors, All Patron Deities, all Guardian Angels, Harmonious Spirits and Energies and Spirits of All Things That Created This House and Home. We greet you and humbly ask that you join in this blessing. And, so it is!

First Circle

Leader: Our first circle is to clear out old energies that may have come in during construction or from other people. We will take our drums and rattles around to every corner of the house opening all closet doors and cupboard doors to clear out the old energy. Go to each door and window, fireplace and other openings, make as much racket as you can, then return here to the hearth altar.

Everyone chants as they go around the house: *Out, out and don't return, what's gone before is here no more.*

Second Circle

The second circle is to purify the home. Let us envision a great Circle of Light spreading out from this candle to all the corners of the property, envisioning the light as pink. *We light this cleansing plant to purify this space.* The home and each room may be purified with sage. If the smoke alarms will go off, bless the water, add a bit of salt and sprinkle it around the house. Go to each door and window, fireplace and other openings, and all the corners with the blessing. Return to the hearth altar.

All: *God bless the corners of this house; the peace of man, the peace of God, the peace of love on all.*

Third Circle

The third circle is for blessing and sealing the home. Envision the Great Circle of Light this time as Purple. Bless the water. *I call on all who are gathered here to bless this water to seal this house with good.*

Go to each door and window, fireplace and other opening and mark upon the opening with the water, blessing and sealing it. Return to the hearth altar.

All: *Only light and good shall dwell, Spirit now shall bless and seal. With this holy water this house is sealed with love and light protecting all within.*

Householder Blessing

Householder lights the second candle. *I light this candle of peace and love. May it protect and shield and guard this home. Let it bring forth happiness and joy, to provide security and abundance, to share in love, friendship and laughter.*

Leader: Bless the oil and anoint the householders, who will then carry the candle to every room and return to the hearth altar.

All: *We bring this candle to light our home in peace, happiness, joy and love.*

Closing

Leader: (Take out and bless the bread, salt, cheese, apple and water. Pour a drop of water on the threshold of the front door saying:)

Guardian Spirits, grant entry to all friends and loved ones and turn aside any that would do harm. Thank you, Holy Ones, for your blessings on this new home. The Circle is now closed. (Return to the hearth altar.)

Dedication

Leader: We dedicate this home to love and understanding. This home is now a place of love. This home is now a place of joy. This home is now a place of friendship. This home is now a place of cooperation. This home is now a place of appreciation. This home is now a place of unity, peace, appreciation, cooperation, friendship, joy, and love. May its life be ever filled with serenity and the consciousness of the unity of all life. And, so it is.

Bury the good luck charms by the front door or put them in a box near the front door. You can also plant a rose bush as a living symbol that this house has been blessed.

Notes: Everyone who has participated shall then eat the apples and drink a sip of water, leaving a portion for the Spirits of the Home. (Take this portion out to feed the birds.)

BUSINESS CLEANSING, BLESSING, AND DEDICATION

Businesses should also be cleansed and blessed every year. This ceremony could be done on the anniversary of the opening or other appropriate time. The business owner(s) and staff should all be involved.

Supplies: Special cloth; salt; water and cups for all participants; oil for blessing; incense or sage; 2 candles; drums, rattles or other noise- makers.

Instructions: set up the altar in the center of the business, placing the other items upon it.

Opening

The owner shall light the first candle on the altar as everyone envisions this light encompassing the building, land and workers with a Golden Light.

We bring to light this guardian flame, to cast all shadows back from whence they came.

Prayer

Leader: *We call upon the Creators of All Life, The Great Spirit, the Keepers of the Four Directions, the Ancestors, All Patron Deities, all Guardian Angels, Harmonious Spirits and Energies and Spirits of All Things That Created This building and land and enliven all the people who work here. We greet you and humbly ask that you join in this blessing. And, so it is!*

First Circle

Our first circle is to clear out old energies that may have come in during construction and set up of this business or from other people. We will take our drums and rattles around to every corner of the business opening all closet doors and cupboard doors to clear out the old energy. Go to each door and window, fireplace and other openings, make as much racket as you can, saying:

All: Out, out and don't return, what's gone before is here no more.

Second Circle

The second circle is for blessing the business. Envision the Circle of Light again, this time envisioning the light as pink. (If appropriate, light the sage and use the smoke to bless the business.) If, the smoke alarms will go off, bless the water, add a bit of salt, and sprinkle it around the building. Bless the water and pour into the cups. Sprinkle the blessed water into every corner of the building and out into the yard.

All: This business is blessed with love and light.

Business Owner Blessing

Business owner lights the second candle. *I light this candle of peace and love. May it protect and shield and guard this business. Let it bring forth happiness and joy, to provide security and abundance to all, to share in love, friendship, and laughter, and prosperity for all who enter here.*

Leader: Blesses the oil and anoints the business owner, who will then carry the candle to every room. *We bring this candle to light this business with peace, happiness, joy and love and prosperity.* Return to the altar.

Third Circle

The third circle is to seal the business for prosperity. Envision the Great Circle of Light, this time as Purple. Taking the blessed water, participants go to each door and window, fireplace and other opening and mark upon the opening sealing it. Return to the altar.

All: With this holy water, I seal this business and service and protect all within.

Blessing Prayer

Leader: *May the Great Spirit of Life bless the corners of this business that all who enter here find answers to their life's questions, gifts of joy and happiness, friendliness and comfort. Bless this business with success and prosperity. May it be a beacon of light to all who can see. Bless the owner and everyone who works here and bless each and every person who enters these doors. And, so it is!*

Closing

Leader: *Guardian Spirits, grant entry to all friends and and turn aside any that would do harm. May the Holy Spirit bless this building and land and all the people who work here that their higher purpose come into being. And so it is and ever shall be!* (Participants pour remaining water over thresholds of front and back doors.)

BLESSING OF A SPACE TO TRANSFORM TRAUMA INTO PEACE

In today's world, not only people but spaces are affected by trauma. The environment retains all the negative energy from the traumatic act and the grief of the people who have been in the space. This ceremony is to help Mother Earth bring harmony and balance back to the place.

Supplies: People with a desire to heal and balance. Candles for everyone and a lighter.

Instructions: Form a Circle of Light, pray for peace, harmony, and balance. Take the Light to all the corners of the space to help Mother Earth heal.

Opening

Leader: We are gathered here in the Circle of Light to pray for the healing of this space. We are here to add comfort to the ground, surround the plants and trees and all beings with love, and add our own light to help heal this part of Mother Earth. We call in the Angels, the Protectors, the Guides, the Higher Selves, the Guardians of this Place, and all Living Things That Dwell Here or Visit.

Let us pray: *Divine and Loving Spirits, Creator of All Life, All the Spirits and Souls Who are Gathered Here, we ask your blessings and protection for this place, a place of joy and happiness. Cleanse it with your Love and Grace, Guard it from outside influences and fill each heart that enters here with Love, the most powerful force in the Universe. We give thanks that your Light surrounds this place of grass and trees, of water and birds, and all other Life that co-exist together in Harmony. May this part of our Mother the Earth be cleansed and sealed with your Holy Spirit. And, so it is.*

You are invited to share your personal prayers at this time. (Allow time for sharing)

Healing Circle of Light

Now, envision a great Healing Light in the center of this circle. It is a powerful light filled with Love and Peace. Watch it expand until it reaches out to your heart. Take hold of a part of the Light and carry it to all the corners of this place and leave it there to shine brightly. The Healing Light cleanses all the negative energy from this space and fills it with Love. Spread the Healing Light over each tree and bush, all living creatures, and over all other objects in this place. When you are finished, return to this Circle.

Candlelight Blessing

We light our candles as a symbol that harmony and balance have returned to this place filling it with the Holy Light of the Divine and healing this part of Mother Earth. With the blessings of the Holy Spirits, we also bless and pray for healing for everyone involved in this situation and all their families. May the Light of God shine in their lives and they be comforted.

Thank you to everyone who helped with this healing. Thank you, Angels, Protectors, Guides, Higher Selves, and Guardians. Thank you, Divine Spirit. We affirm that this place is now cleansed and protected by the Light of God. And, so it is.

Light candles and all sing together a peace song or "Amazing Grace."

PEACE POLE PRAYER GATHERINGS

Our spiritual community is a part of the establishing of Peace Poles around the world, of which there are over 200,000 in 197 countries. We began a project to erect 100 Peace Poles in 2016. As of this writing, we have 32. What started out as a project just for our city has expanded to other cities and countries. We have three Peace Poles in Nepal, one in Kansas, and several in outlying communities all part of this ongoing project.

We put up the first Peace Pole in 2007 in the Ute Indian Park across from the Ute Indian Museum, the only museum in the United States dedicated solely to one tribe. This Peace Pole has "May peace prevail on earth" written in eight different languages, honoring the people who came to this area and the five continents of the world. During the year we sponsor prayer gatherings at the Peace Pole to pray for the healing of Mother Earth and for peace for the world. We gather at the equinoxes, the solstices, Earth Day, the International Day of Peace, and other special occasions.

This is a sample ceremony we adapt to fit the theme of the season or the celebration. We bring our drums and instruments to lift the energy. Sometimes we do a Dance of Universal Peace, have a flag ceremony honoring all the nations of the world, do a teaching such as the Universal Peace Shield, or simply sit in meditative silence.

This ceremony could be used for any prayer gathering in any location.

CEREMONY OF NATIONS

This ceremony is to honor the nations of the world and pray for peace. Small flags or paper flags may be used to create a mandala around the Peace Pole. The purpose of this ceremony is to expand the awareness of peace to include other nations and other peoples and to remind us that we are all part of the Great Circle of Life.

Supplies: Flags of different nations; sage for smudging; drums and other instruments.

Instructions: Participants are invited to smudge themselves before entering the circle. During the ceremony they are invited to choose a flag and bless the country before setting it into the Peace Mandala. The ceremony ends with a Sufi dance.

Opening

Leader: Welcome to our Prayer Gathering for Peace and the healing of Mother Earth. Today we are also blessing the nations of the world for peace.

Our Peace Prayer today is by Baha'u'llah, founder of the Baha'i faith:

> *"We desire the good of the world and the happiness of the nations that the bonds of affection and unity between the sons of men should be strengthened... what harm is there in this?... these fruitless strifes, these ruinous wars shall pass away, and the 'Most Great Peace' shall come."*

Because we stand on sacred ground, we begin each gathering here in this Medicine Wheel with a prayer to the Four Directions. Please face East.

Spirit of the East, we ask that you be with us as we pray for peace on earth. Show us that each day should begin with peace. Aho. Turn South.

Spirit of the South, be with us as we look upon your snow-covered mountains, help us remember that peace is strength not weakness. Aho. Turn West.

Spirit of the West, be with us and remind us as the sun goes down and night comes that in that darkness peace lights the way. Aho. Turn North.

Spirit of the North, be with us and help us contemplate peace before we take action. Help us to be quiet and know that peace is always in our hearts. Aho. Turn Center.

Creator of All Life, be with us and show us the way to Peace. Aho.

Mother Earth, be with us as we pledge to work for peace for all your children. Aho.

Heart of My Own Heart, please work with me to take right action in peace and to speak only the words of peace. Aho.

We come together to pray for peace on earth. People all around the world are praying for peace every day. To honor our brothers and sisters of other countries, I invite you to come forward and choose a flag and place it in a circle around the Peace Pole. We are creating a mandala of nations. Before you place the flag in the circle, bless it and please read the country to which it belongs. We will then respond, *"Let peace prevail in the country of (Name)."* Keep placing the flags until all of them are in the Peace Mandala.

Sealing of the Peace

Leader: (When the flags are all placed, the group repeats the peace prayer.): *May Peace be with all the Indigenous Nations, May Peace be in all Industrial Nations, May Peace be with all the other Regions of the World, May Peace Prevail On Earth!*

We release the Spirits of the Four Directions and express our gratitude for their presence at this peace gathering. Thank you, Spirits of East, South, West, and North. Thank you, Great Spirit and thank you, our Mother the Earth. Peace prevails on earth and among all people. And, so it is.

Sufi Heart Dance for Peace

To conclude our ceremony let us form a circle, join hands, and do the Sufi Heart Dance. Sufi Heart Dance Refrain - (*I am Peace. You are Peace. We are Peace.*)

Directions: Form a circle holding hands. Take a few moments to visualize the heart of Mother Earth in the center (or the Heart of the Divine). With the first phrase the circle bends into the center to the left, dipping each heart into the Heart in the Center of the Circle. With the second phrase, the circle bends to the right dipping the hearts. With the third phrase, the circle bends forward in the center. Repeat the bending and chanting as a smooth flow until the Leader feels a shift in the energy and the Circle is moving as one body in peace.

Leader: Take a moment and feel this peace we have created here. Anchor it into your heart so that any time you need to feel peaceful, you will remember this moment of peace. (Silence). In these next few moments send this peace out to all the nations of the world from the Peace Mandala in the center of our Circle.

Closing

Let us close with this peace prayer:

Peace prevails on Earth.
Peace prevails in our hearts.
Peace prevails in our families.
Peace prevails in our community.
Peace prevails in our nation.
Peace prevails on Earth.
And, so it is.

Creating Your Own Ceremonies

Catharina Bates

CREATING YOUR OWN CEREMONIES

Ceremonies are very personal rituals to honor the great Mystery of Life, to honor the sacredness of your life, and the sacredness of all Creation. Ceremonies are living prayers. The Creator does not care what name you call the great Mystery. Be guided in your ceremony by what your heart and spirit direct you to do and know it is the proper ceremony for that time. All ceremony is done with humbleness, respect, reverence, honor, and gratitude.

Here are a few suggestions to consider when creating your own ceremonies.

Intention –To experience more deeply the sacredness of your life, focus on your reason for doing the ceremony.

Purpose – Choose a clear and single spiritual purpose for the ceremony.

Preparation – Prepare yourself. Gather all the symbols and supplies before the ceremony, including the special cloth. You can add a candle, symbols of the elements, a religious symbol or other symbols that speak to your own sacredness.

Acknowledgement – Gratitude and acknowledgment of the Great Mystery, the essence of Spirit that is beyond, and is called by many names, begins each ceremony.

Gratitude –Express sincere gratitude from mind, heart and soul which brings you into alignment for the ceremony.

The Call – Open yourself to the sacred. Relax into the world beyond this one and feel the presence of the Divine on a deeper level. Spend some time in the quietness.

Ritual – Let your senses reach beyond the physical world to the world of spirit. Be willing to receive and accept the messages from beyond.

Prayers – Speak your prayers from your heart.

Listen – Hear the voice of the sacred no matter what form it comes in, it might be a whisper, a feeling, a symbol.

Dedication – Renew your commitment to walk the sacred path of your life.

Closing Prayer –Seal your ceremony with gratitude for your life, your inspirations, and the love of the Divine.

Note: If you want to add ceremony to your spiritual practice, honor your ceremonial items by keeping them wrapped together in your special ceremony cloth in a safe and honored place.

WEDDING CEREMONIES

Marriage, binding two people together into one life, is an important landmark of life and should be marked with sacred ceremony. Couples can make the wedding ceremony more personal by adding special scripture readings, poems that express their deep feelings, and music that speaks to their souls. There are many resources for couples today to help them write their own ceremony. The wishes and feelings of each party should be included in this first ceremony they make together to express their spiritual commitment. Family wishes should also be considered.

Wedding ceremonies are held in churches, synagogues, temples, parks, hotels, resorts, on the beach or in the mountains, in backyards, and in government offices. In some states the couple simply registers with the county clerk and they are immediately married. Wherever the ceremony is held, it should be marked with prayers and blessings for it is a sacred time in the lives of the two people who are making the commitment of marriage.

Meaning of Marriage

The meaning of marriage is a coming together with integrity and commitment. It is a time to honor the Divine Spirit within each other and to foster the greatest possible spiritual growth. What is most essential today in marriage is honesty, truth, and love. Truth and love cannot be separated, they walk hand in hand. Marriage allows the Truth of who we really are to come forth and shine.

The purpose of human love is to awaken love for the Divine. The doorway of human love is a perfectly acceptable channel to experience the broader realities, for love is love. As people learn to love, the very act of loving opens a greater understanding of how to give love.

Love cannot be exhausted for love is all that exists. Love is the universal communication. It is the energy that created the universe and is the energy that continues to move through all of creation. The Divine Spirit is Love. All matter is formed by this Love. The physical world holds together with this Love.

True marriage is formed through the everyday acts of kindness, consideration, honor and respect. True marriage is the last field of relationship before we reach for the stars. We cannot reach the stars without understanding Love.

Order of a Wedding Ceremony

The following is a traditional order of a Western wedding ceremony. Choose which elements are meaningful for you to include in your ceremony. Many couples write their own vows for the ceremony. The readings are meaningful for the couple and their families.

The marriage ceremony is held in a sacred space and in a sacred and reverent manner for it is a spiritual commitment between the couple and is holy.

Music
Lighting of Candles
Seating of the Groom's Mother and Father
Seating of the Bride's Mother
Special Solo
Entrance of Groom, Groomsmen and Officiant
Bridesmaids Entrance
Flower Girl and Ring Bearer
Entrance of Bride and Escort (Father)

Welcome by Officiant
Purpose of Gathering
Words about Marriage
Special Reading(s)
The Charge (agreement to the commitment)
Exchange of Vows
Exchange of Rings
Lighting of Unity Candle by Couple
Pronouncement of Marriage
Sealing of Marriage
Introduction of Mr. and Mrs.

Exit of Bride and Groom
Exit of Attendants
Escort of Bride's Parents
Escort of Groom's Parents

HOLY UNION CEREMONIES

A Holy Union Ceremony is similar to a traditional marriage ceremony, except there may be two brides or two grooms. It is another form of sacred marriage and should be entered into reverently. The order of service is the same as the traditional wedding ceremony and is celebrated with family and friends. (Check the laws concerning marriage in your state.)

RENEWAL OF MARRIAGE VOWS

Couples who have been married for several years may choose to re-commit to each other through holding a renewal ceremony. It is also a sacred time honoring the years the couple has been together and dedicating the years to come. It is a time for family and friends to come together and celebrate the blessings of love and marriage. The order of service for the traditional marriage may be used with words of re-dedication in place of the vows.

SUGGESTIONS FOR ADDITIONAL CEREMONIES TO CREATE

There are many other opportunities to celebrate with sacred ceremony. Any event that marks a milestone in life, a new beginning, or an ending and releasing. Gratitude is always a good ceremony for everyday events, beloved family members, and good friends. When we can experience all of creation as a blessing, then we can become whole again.

PERSONAL
- Recovering from an illness
- Starting a new job or business
- Welcoming home a person who has been gone a long time
- Starting medical treatments
- Having surgery
- Engagement to be married
- Reconciliation
- Personal success
- Blessing the self after a struggle
- Blessing a new computer system

FAMILY
- Moving to a new house or state
- First day of school
- Graduation
- Starting college
- Blessing a new car
- Welcoming new relatives for a blended family
- Blessing the grandparents
- Blessing the parents
- Blessing the family pets
- Welcoming home from a honeymoon

COMMUNITY

- Blessing sports teams
- Celebrating a community
- Blessing a new subdivision
- Blessing the opening of the local farmers market
- Blessing the schools
- Blessing the teachers
- Blessing the parks
- Blessing the downtown or center of the community

APPENDIX

PRAYERS TO THE FOUR DIRECTIONS

O East, the direction of new beginnings. Help us to be open to the new beginnings in each day as the sun rises over the world. Be with us now and give us peace.

O South, the direction of summer. Help us to be more tolerant of our brothers and sisters as we grow into the fullness of life, living together in peace. Be with us now and give us peace.

O West, the direction of Wisdom. Help us to share our Truth in wise ways to bring more understanding to ourselves and others. Be with us now and give us peace.

O North, the direction of contemplation. Help us to release the old ways and make way for the new ways as we prepare ourselves for new beginnings. Be with us now and give us peace.

Turn center - O Grandfather Sky, help us see a bigger world where peace can dwell. Be with us now and give us peace.

O Grandmother Earth, help us to care for ourselves, to care for you and all the life that you nurture. Be with us now and give us peace.

O Heart of my own Heart, may we always be open to the teachings of the directions and the Great Spirit. Be with us now and give us peace.

PRAYERS TO RELEASE THE FOUR DIRECTIONS

Thank you, Spirit of the East, for being here with us, for opening our eyes and hearts to peace and healing.

Turn South. Thank you, Spirit of the South, for being here with us, for opening our hearts and minds to peace and healing.

Turn West. Thank you, Spirit of the West for being here with us, for opening our minds and souls to peace and healing.

Turn North. Thank you, Spirit of the North, for being here with us, for opening our souls and all of our being to peace and healing.

Turn Center. Thank you, Creator, for all your blessings. Let us walk with moccasins of beauty upon the earth and bring peace to all our relations.

Go now in peace and walk in beauty.

SAMPLE MODERN SEDER MENU
(The potluck menu served at the Spiritual Awareness Center)

Matzah Ball Soup
Matzah Crackers
Meatloaf
Potatoes Au Gratin
Spring Vegetable Dish or Quiche
Apple Salad – Charoset (see recipe following)
Deviled or Pickled Eggs
Brownies
Sparkling Juice

CHAROSET (Apple Salad):

Apples cut into bite-size pieces, raisins, almonds or other nuts, cinnamon, lemon juice, and sugar to sweeten if needed. Combine all ingredients, use grape juice as dressing.

BIBLIOGRAPHY

Anastasio, Janet; Bevilacqua, Michelle; and, Peters, Stephanie. *The Everything Wedding Book*. Avon, MA: Adams Media Corporation, 2000.

Bainbridge, John. *Huna Magic*. Los Angeles: Barnhart Press, 1988

Boone, J. Allen. *Kinship with All Life*. New York: Harper & Row Publishers, 1976.

Campanelli, Pauline. *Wheel of the Year: Living the Magical Life. USA: 1990.*

Driver, Tom F. *Magic Ritual: Our Need for Liberating Rites that Transform Our Lives and Our Communities*. San Francisco: Harper, 1991.

Emmanuel, complied by Rodegast, Pat and Stanton, Judith. *Emmanuel's Book II: The Choice for Love*. New York: Bantam Books, 1989.

Emoto, Masaru. *The Secret Life of Water*. New York: Atria Books, 2005.

Farmer, Steven D. *Sacred Ceremony: How to Create Ceremonies for Healing, Transitions, and Celebrations*. Hay House, 2002.

Gibran, Kahlil. *The Prophet*. New York: Alfred A. Knopp, Inc, 1923

Hay, Louise L. *Heart Thoughts: A Treasury of Inner Wisdom*. Santa Monica, CA: Hay House, Inc., 1990.

Horn, Gabriel. *The Book of Ceremonies: A Native Way of Honoring and Living the Sacred*. Navato, CA: New World Library, 2000.

Scheinerman, Rabbi Amy. *Seder Service*. www.chabat.org, 2000.

Spangler, David. *Festivals in the New Age*. Scotland: Findhorn, 1975

Storm, Hyemeyohsts. *Seven Arrows*. New York: Ballantine, 1972.

Sacraments of the Church of Truth. Pasadena, CA.

Zambucka, Kristin. *Ano, Ano, the Seed*. Honolulu, HI: Mana Publishing Co., 1978.

Printed in the United States
By Bookmasters